THE IMPOSSIBLE CHANGE

Lesbian to Missionary

For nothing is impossible
with God. Luke 1:37

Blessings,
Priscilla Maward

For nothing is impossible
with God. Luke 1:37

Blessings,

THE IMPOSSIBLE CHANGE

Lesbian to Missionary

Priscilla Navaroli

XULON PRESS ELITE

Some of the names in this story have been changed to protect the identity of the individuals.

Warning: This book's content may be triggering to some readers as it contains explicit content pertaining to sexual abuse.

Xulon Press Elite
2301 Lucien Way #415
Maitland, FL 32751
407.339.4217
www.xulonpress.com

The Impossible Change: Lesbian to Missionary
© 2021 by Priscilla Navaroli

Unless otherwise indicated, Scripture quotations taken from the *New King James Version (NKJV)*. Copyright © 1982 by Thomas Nelson, Inc. Used by permission. All rights reserved.

Scripture quotations taken from the *Holy Bible, New Living Translation (NLT)*. Copyright ©1996, 2004, 2007 by Tyndale House Foundation. Used by permission of Tyndale House Publishers, Inc.

Edited by Xulon Press

Printed in the United States of America

Paperback ISBN-13: 978-1-66281-3-290
Ebook ISBN-13: 978-1-66281-3-306

Dedication

I want to dedicate this book to Jesus Christ, my Lord, and Savior. Thank You for Your grace, Your love, and Your mercy. For saving a wretch like me and calling me into Your marvelous light; and using me according to Your will and purpose.

I also want to dedicate this book to my mom Luci. You loved me and provided for me the best that you could. I appreciate that with all my heart. But most of all, thank you for all the prayers you sent up to Heaven on my behalf and for NEVER giving up on me during those thirty years I stumbled around in the dark. Thank you, I love you, mom.

To my husband, Raymond Navaroli Jr., my Kingsman redeemer. Thank you for allowing me to experience being a wife. I love you and miss you. -P

Acknowledgements

ammy, "my Cherianne," for being the best sister and my best friend. Thank you for doing your best always to protect me.

Pastor Darla Weaver, thank you for the six years of being my mentor. You and Pastor Randy took a chance on me and believed in me even when I didn't believe in myself. You helped me mature into the Christian woman I am today. The five years I spent on staff at LSCC will always be treasured and remembered.

Nicole Donoho, without you, this book would not have been possible. Thank you for all your hard work.

Table of Contents

Introduction

*I*t all started on Saturday, April 23, 2011. I would have spent it just like any other Saturday, except this Saturday just so happened to be the day before Easter Sunday. Which meant there had been much anticipation leading up to this weekend: the boat, the lake, the sun, the beer. I'm sure it had been the only thing on my mind leading up to this weekend.

What other way was there to spend a holiday? I drove over to Walmart and bought some beer because every holiday needs beer. Especially when you're on a boat at the lake, that evening, I got the boat ready for the morning. I also made sure the beer and snacks were ready to go. Preparing all these things the morning of departure is for amateurs. When you have it all prepared to go the night before, it maximizes the time you have for relaxation the next day. And I was all about maximizing that!

When I walked outside the next morning to get the boat hooked up, conditions were less than favorable. The wind was blowing, and it seemed a bit breezier than we had anticipated. Christy, my partner of three years at the time, and I decided we should wait until noon to see if the wind would die down. Lake Conroe is not a lake you wanted to be on when it was windy. The waters get choppy, and the lake creates white caps.

By mid-afternoon Easter Sunday, the increased winds blew away all my plans of relaxing on the lake. I put my boat back and sulked, just a little, over my ruined plans. I'd been looking forward to spending a lovely day on the lake. What else was there to do on Easter Sunday? Go to church? Not this gal. I'd paid all those attendance dues when I was younger, and there was no way I'd ever go back. Easter was just another holiday to kick back with a twelve-pack, which is a lot more acceptable when you're relaxing at the lake. Kicking back with a twelve-pack in your living room just doesn't have the same appeal. It's a bit more depressing than relaxing.

Later that afternoon, after accepting the lake wouldn't be happening today, Christy and I retreated to my favorite places in the house, my TV room. I had a big-screen television and three top-of-the-line leather reclining movie chairs. Since I am a big movie buff, that was a great place to escape. Not quite as good as my lake plans, but it would do for today.

This particular Sunday, we decided to watch *The Passion of the Christ,* directed by Mel Gibson. Once again, I find my plans going sideways. I can tell you for sure, watching *this* movie would not have been my idea. Not only was I anti-church-going, but I was also agnostic and slightly leaning more towards atheism at this time of my life. I had even begun reading books about Scientology. There seemed to be a lot of talk about it, and so far, I was enjoying what Rob Hubbard, the founder, had to say. I was content to stay as far away from Christians as I possibly could. My thoughts were, "If you stay away from me, I will stay away from you."

However, Christy was more on the believing side and would attend church whenever she visited her family. I'm sure she probably had a lot to do with deciding on the movie that day. She may have even thrown in a 'since it's Easter' comment to smooth it over. As if that made a difference to me.

As the movie started, I had no feelings one way or another about it. I had seen it before, and I wasn't moved by it whatsoever. But something was different this time. Here I thought I was about to watch a movie just to pass the time. Never once did I suspect it would wind up changing my whole life from that day forward.

The Passion began with Jesus in The Garden of Gethsemane. He was praying for the cup that He has to bear to be taken away from Him. *Here's an idea, Jesus, just don't do it. No means no, and you do what you want with your life.* He obviously didn't hear my thoughts through the screen. This man was sweating blood in complete anguish. And for what? I'm not a heartless person. I felt terrible for Jesus's character. He looked like He was in distress, but still, it meant nothing to me. This actor was just the same as any other actor in a movie.

I know some people saw this movie playing out as real-life events, but it was just another movie to me. I didn't believe in the Bible. It was just a book with a copyright date written so many years ago. It's been translated from one language to another and probably lost a lot of validity in the process. That's what I had believed all of my adult life, and at this point- I was 45 years old- nothing was going to change my mind.

At the end of His prayer, He says, "Nevertheless not My will, but Yours be done." *What does that mean? Why is He doing this?* I watch as the chief priest officers take Jesus away, and still, I have no understanding of why He is doing what He is doing. He didn't break any laws that I can see, but here He is, walking away peacefully. At one point, He stood before Pilate, and the Roman soldiers are given instructions to flog Jesus. They take him and shackle His wrists to a stump. Then, they start to scourge, or whip, Him with the cat-of-nine-tails, which consisted of multiple leather straps tied together with hooks on them that would tear out His flesh.

During this scourging, I became uneasy with every stroke as I watched His flesh being torn from His body. But I still didn't know, or rather understand, why He was going through this.

Yes, I grew up in a religious home. As I said before, I paid my attendance dues. I learned about Jesus. I knew He died on the cross. I had heard all the stories growing up, and I knew what the celebration of Easter was all about, or so I thought. However, I had never been taught grace and mercy. Jesus died on the cross for my sins. My horrible, wretched unforgivable sins. That's where the spotlight landed on the stories I was told–my sins.

My mom was always shoving Christianity down my throat verse by verse. I was a sinner in her eyes, and I was going to hell for everything I did. The worst of those things being the lifestyle I choose to live. Why would I want to believe in a God that was always ready to strike me down? No, ma'am, she could have her judgmental God. I wanted nothing to do with Him.

There was this moment in that scouring scene where Jesus' eyes make direct contact with the camera. It was just for a split second, but it was the split second that He needed to speak directly to me. Many people throughout my life would try and talk to me about Jesus, but I would not listen. I would have a fit if someone tried to preach to me. My response was, "When you start paying my taxes, I will listen to you about your Jesus, but until then, keep your beliefs to yourself." It was a quick way to shut people up since I knew they weren't going to pay my taxes.

Years of avoiding Jesus talks were tossed aside in one split second of eye contact with a movie actor. Because at that moment, I heard the sweetest, most loving voice I have ever heard in my entire life. It was the sound of unconditional love, and it pierced right through the stone-cold walls of my heart. At that moment, I heard ever so clearly, "I did this for you."

With every strike of that whip, "I did this for you." As he's walking to Calvary, "I did this for you."

Since I knew what I was hearing, I asked Christy, "Do you hear that?"

She said, "Hear what?"

I said, "Never mind." The last thing a sane person wants to do is admit they hear voices.

As Jesus walked to Calvary, I could feel something tapping on my heart. It felt like it was being chiseled, and it ached.

By this time, my eyes were overflowing with tears to the point where they had begun to run down the sides of my cheeks. I brushed them off casually so that Christy wouldn't see me crying. I couldn't let her see the way this movie was affecting me. Absolutely not! She knew what I thought and believed about religion, especially Christianity, and I wasn't going to let this movie change how I felt.

Around the time Jesus got to the cross, I couldn't wait for the movie to be over. Every pound of each nail, "I did this for you." I didn't know what was going on inside of me. I thought I was going nuts because I knew someone was talking to me, but I didn't know who. Or at least I didn't want to admit who it might be at the time. Really. I didn't believe in this stuff. But yet the voice continued. Finally, Jesus dies on the cross, and I'm all turned around inside, not sure what to think. He raises from the dead, ascends to heaven; movie over. *Glad that's over.*

I had no idea it would only be the beginning. Later that evening, as I began to fall asleep, I saw those eyes and hear the voice say, "I did this for you."

You have got to be kidding me!! I spent most of the night tossing and turning, trying to forget the incident. But the next morning, when I woke up, there it was once more. "I did this for you."

Oh, come on!!

I drove to work. And what do I hear clear as if someone is sitting in my passenger seat? "I did this for you."

Seriously!!

Finally, I gave in to the voice, "I don't know who you are but stop it."

This went on for three days before I eventually stopped hearing the voice. Had I been a Christian at the time, this would have been one of those "praise the Lord" moments. I'm hearing Jesus personally; this is so great. But that wasn't me. I was glad things had quieted down and returned to normal.

During that time, I was a contractor for FedEx Ground. I owned three delivery trucks and several zip codes in the state of Texas. The week following Easter, I decided I was tired of listening to music. I'd generally spend 10 hours a day in a truck listening to music- country, soft rock, classic rock, and every other genre that's out there. Music was my background noise as I was in and out of the truck delivering packages. But, for whatever reason, I was tired of it all this week and wanted to listen to some talk radio. I came across a radio station talking about money. I liked money. So, I parked the dial on that station.

The man speaking, who I found out later to be Pastor David Mitchell, was talking about investments in stocks. I was a very materialistic person, always after the next big thing to satisfy my soul. And since most of those next big things required money, he had my interest...until he brought up the Bible. He brought up the Parable of the Talents, and immediately I changed the channel. I shook my head in disbelief. He was doing so good; why'd he go and ruin it with that Bible talk? I'm sure there was an eye roll and probably a swear word before returning to my deliveries.

The next morning, I came across the same station, and once again, this man was talking about investments. So, again I parked the channel there thinking that yesterday was a fluke. Unbeknownst to me, I was listening to a Christian radio station, and this man was a pastor. Yeah, the joke was on me. In this lesson, the investor brought up the parable of the widow's mite. The money talk is still good, so I listened for a few more minutes before turning it off.

Well, come Monday the following week, around the same time, I once again come across the station, and the pastor was once again talking about investments. I didn't realize the station had this time of day dedicated to him each weekday. This time I decided I enjoyed listening to him, so I would just ignore the Bible stuff when it came up. And besides, since I was going in and out of my truck making deliveries, I would miss most of it anyway. I left it on the station and went about my day.

I went through a few stops listening to my investment preacher and ignoring the Bible stuff. It seemed to be working out pretty well until I returned to the truck, and they had a real preacher actually preaching! It was Charles Stanley. I finally realized it was a church station and said, "No, no, I ain't listening *to YOU!*" I knew his type, or at least I thought I did. Those religious folks who wanted to bash me over the head with the Bible telling me every single thing I was 'doing wrong.'

The next day, I was once again sucked into the investment guy's segment. Like they say, 'money talks' especially to me. I grabbed the good points and ignored the Bible stuff. Since I already knew it was coming, it wasn't as hard to ignore. We're going along pretty well until I return to my truck after a delivery only to discover Charles Stanley has taken it over again. I reached for the button to switch the channel and heard the voice say, "Listen." I knew that voice. It was the "I did this for you." voice. If I turned the station now, I'd probably have to hear it the rest of the day.

"Ok fine!" I said audibly, responding to the voice of someone I couldn't see, "But if he mentions my lifestyle, I will never listen again."

Anyone walking by my truck that day probably would have thought I had lost my mind. I wasn't quite sure I hadn't. But from that day forward and for a whole week, I listened to Charles Stanley every morning after my investment preacher. Something started to feel different, and his words were moving me. One day as I was driving to my next delivery, Charles asked if anyone wanted to receive Jesus Christ as their Savior. If they did, then they should pray with him.

Once again, the voice speaks. This time He says, "Pull over."

I got a little nervous. Obviously, this voice didn't know me very well or at least didn't understand religion. "I can't...my life... I'm gay."

He said, "Pull over."

So, I pulled my FedEx truck over on the side of the road and prayed the sinner's prayer with Charles Stanley. When I was done, I found myself bawling harder than I have ever cried in my entire life. I was heaving and heaving. I saw all my sins flash in front of me. My mom told me many times that I was a sinner throughout the years because of the rebellious choices and the lesbian lifestyle I chose to live. I always threw it back at her, "No, you're the sinner; I have character defects." I had always turned things back on her because of the hypocrisy I watched in her life. If liking girls was not something I should do, it was obviously a character defect, not a sin. Not my problem; God broke my mold. But, right there, in my FedEx truck, I knew that I was, in fact, a sinner. There was no denying it. There was a holy God of whom I was far from. But unlike all the times I had been called out as a sinner, this time was different. This time, the spotlight didn't hover over my sins, pointing out just how wrong I was in every way. Instead, it focused on a God who loved that sinner-me. Why? Why would He love wretched me?

When I had finished crying, I wiped the snot off my nose and got myself together. I immediately said out loud. "Because of what you did for me, I will give up my lifestyle for you." From that moment on, I listened to that station twelve hours a day, five days a week. I had been searching for this kind of love and acceptance my entire life!

But maybe I should rewind to the beginning. All you've seen so far is a 45-year-old lesbian giving her life to Jesus. That would be like watching the end of Shawshank Redemption, seeing Andy Dufresne walk on the beach with his friend Red and thinking it was a great movie. You would have no idea of the struggle this man had to endure having spent twenty years in prison for a crime he didn't commit. No idea of everything that led him to the moment you were now witnessing.

To get a better picture, let's go back far enough so you can understand just how little I wanted to do with God and

Christianity. Far enough to let you see where the bitterness and anger were planted and flourished like weeds choking out all that was beautiful. There were so many different segments in my life that impacted the person I became. I'd like to take a moment and walk you through each of those.

Chapter 1

A Broken Foundation

M y parents Valentino and Luci, were teenagers when they met and fell in love. One night, while they were on a date, they fell asleep in the backseat of a car. My mom was terrified to return home after being out all night with her boyfriend, so she did the *logical* thing and convinced him to elope with her the next morning. Here they were, seventeen and nineteen, married simply because they were out all night with each other. It wasn't like they didn't love each other, but with that kind of start, it's not hard to see doom on the horizon. I believe this decision seemed *logical* to my mom because of the strict household she grew up in. It was better to jump into marriage than come home to face some consequences. My mother was always considered the rebellious one in her family. Guess the apple didn't fall far from the tree, mom!

My sister Tammy was born a year later, and eighteen months after that, I came along. At that time, my parents were now twenty and twenty-two. Sometime before I was three, things began getting rocky between them. I've asked my parents what happened back then, and they both tell very different stories. My mom says he cheated on her, while my dad says she wanted to be wild and left him. Still to this day, I'm not sure what truly happened between them. They got divorced when I was three and shortly before my twin brothers were born. My dad thought he might be their father, he always wanted boys, but my mom told him they were not his. To this day, we're still not sure who their father is.

The earliest memories of my childhood were of us living with my grandmother in Earlimart, California, a tiny town located in the San Joaquin Valley around Central California. It was a small two-bedroom with an outhouse. For this reason, my mom would keep a pot next to the bed when it got dark in case we had to pee. Instead of walking across the yard to the bathroom, we'd just use the pee pot at night. The shower was a nozzle in the wall. It had a cement floor that was rough like a sidewalk. I suppose it could have been worse; at least there was warm water. We had no idea we were poor compared to some people's standards.

Grandma was a huge contributor to our "rich" lifestyle. She would be up early in the morning, making homemade tortillas. Tammy and I would always get the first ones right off the griddle with butter on them. It makes my mouth water just thinking about her cooking. We'd take walks to the fruit stand down the street and pick out some fresh fruit. Oh, the smells of oranges, peaches, strawberries, and nectarines bring back so many good memories. We'd ride our bikes all over the neighborhood and play for hours outside while Grandma did yardwork or repairs on the house. We'd watch her favorite show, Hawaii 5-0, on her plastic-covered furniture because 'it was new.'

One day, I mentioned how I wished we had a treehouse, and my Grandma made it happen. That's how cool she was! She was 55 when she built us that treehouse. Now that I'm an adult, I realize it wasn't really a treehouse. It was only a few slats of 2x4's scattered here and there so we wouldn't fall out of the tree. But to Tammy and me, it was amazing! It was built with love. We thought we were awesome in our new treehouse—the luckiest kids in the world.

But things weren't always good at Grandma's house. She and mom would fight about mom's choice to hang out at dance clubs. Eventually, my mom must have decided she had enough because she packed up all four of us children and moved into an old garage, not the converted type either—just four walls where you park your car kind of garage. We moved two more times until we found ourselves back at Grandma's house; this time, we lived in a tiny Airstream trailer parked on the back of her property. I wasn't sure why we had moved so often, but I was glad to be back at Grandma's.

All was well until mom, once again, could no longer deal with Grandma nagging her, so we moved again. By this time, she had married Moises Murillo because he had the same last name as my dad. (No, before you ask, they weren't related.) This would ensure that her kids had the same last name since she had given the twins my dad's last name. (Even though she still denied they were his.) Moises wasn't in the picture long, though. Mom left Moises, packed our bags, and moved us to Porterville- 25 miles away. At least we got my sister Lisa from that brief marriage.

As a child, I was very close to my mom. Whenever my mom would leave the house, she had to take me with her because if she didn't, I would cry until she got back. I was the kid who would hide behind my mother whenever we'd meet new people. I'd peek around her with curiosity but stay there until I was comfortable enough to move beside her. With that being said, it's no surprise that my first traumatic life experience came on the very first day of kindergarten.

Here's my mom walking this timid introverted child into the classroom. I was petrified; I had an older sister; I knew what was about to happen. This woman was going to abandon me here with strangers- all day! She walked me up to the teacher, Mrs. Widerman, who bent down to greet me, "What is your name?"

"Linky." I quietly replied.

My mom looked at her, laughed a little, and said, "No, her name is Priscilla."

Priscilla? Who the hell is Priscilla? I had never even heard that name in my entire five years of life. At that moment, my world literally exploded as my mom bent down, looked me in the eye, and said, "Your name is Priscilla."

Great, not only is she about to abandon me with all these kids and this strange lady I don't even know, but now she's changing my name. And right there, at five years old, I struggled with my first identity crisis. I didn't know who this Priscilla was, but she ain't me. As I'm standing there with tears in my eyes, mom says, "Linky is your nickname." *What is a nickname?*

Needless to say, kindergarten was a struggle. Do you think I responded when the teacher called on Priscilla? No. It took me quite a while to get used to being called "Priscilla," especially since I was still "Linky" at home and everywhere else, for that matter. Not to mention the fact that the teacher tries to teach you how to spell your name. Guess what? Priscilla is not an easy name to spell!

Thankfully my best cousin, Isaac, being the same age as me, was in my class. I stuck to him like glue. I loved Isaac so much. When my mom abandoned me in kindergarten, he was the only one I knew, so it made our bond that much tighter, and I became a tomboy. Tammy and our cousin Susie would play with dolls and do all the girlie stuff while Isaac and I would build forts and play with army men. Every once in a while, Tammy would convince me to play dolls, but I loved skateboarding, sports, and all things masculine. Whenever mom would buy me a doll, put bows in my hair, or try to put a dress on me, I would cry. I remember she bought me a Baby Chrissy for Christmas one year. I drew on her face and cut off all her hair. Eventually, she gave in and let me have corduroy pants, t-shirts, and all the marbles, army men, and athletic stuff I wanted to play with. I was so happy we had finally come to an understanding of each other. Speaking of girlie things, it wasn't until first grade when I finally started getting used to my new name, Priscilla.

Some of my earliest experiences might seem silly or insignificant at the moment. Did a nickname really scar me for the rest of my life? Maybe not, but it sure didn't lay a solid foundation for success. To understand why I'm walking you through these early memories, you need to know the importance of how to chain an elephant. Yes, an elephant!

See, if you want to chain an elephant, you don't go to an adult elephant and strap a chain to its leg; it will easily break free from its bondage. Instead, you take a baby elephant and chain it to a post. Since it is only a baby, you don't even have to use a shackle; you can use a rope. The reason any kind of strap will do is that the exercise is more psychological than physical. That tiny elephant grows up knowing it can never go farther than the rope will allow. It will grow up to be one of the mightiest mammals on the planet but not wander farther than the length of its bondage. Why? Because it's not the chain itself that binds it but the chain that develops in its mind.

Our minds are impressionable. We are brilliant beings, and yet we allow ourselves to be limited by bondage applied throughout our lives. My early childhood was the foundation of my bondage. I didn't ask for my parents to get divorced, but that certainly altered the way I saw relationships and marriage in the future. I didn't ask to watch my mom and Grandma argue all the time. But seeing it set the standard for 'normal' mother/ daughter behavior in my mind. Growing up, I just thought we moved around a lot. Little did I know this was a trait that I would adopt when I wanted to run away from situations in my life without facing them and dealing with them.

See, when we refuse to recognize and address the things that happened in our life, whether they were by our choices or the choices of others, we are refusing to acknowledge the bondage we may be subject to.

One of my favorite childhood memories from living with my Grandma is when Tammy and I would tear pictures from our coloring book, take water, and stick them on rubber balls to make crystal balls. We'd pretend to see into the future. Isn't that something all of us long to do? Know what the future holds?

The future is full of so many promises, so much abundance. However, just as it was impossible for me and Tammy to gaze into those solid rubber balls plastered with coloring pages, it is also impossible for us to realistically gaze into our future when our past has so clouded it. An elephant cannot merely forget the rope that held it back. It must be retrained to know its own strength and set its mind free from the cage that held it. As Christians, we are called to do the same. Our pasts cannot be buried, covered up, or ignored. Instead, we must expose them and submit ourselves to God for reprogramming. He's the only one who can help us understand our own strength and set our minds free from the cage that holds it. I often tell people, "I don't want to forget where I came from because I might also forget what God has done."

> *"So, Christ has truly set us free. Now make sure that you stay free, and don't get tied up again in slavery to the law." Galatians 5:1 NLT*

God has a whole new normal for us to live by. When we get saved, He wants us to reset to factory settings by reprogramming our minds. But here I am, jumping to the remodel when we've not even built you a picture of the first house. The foundation for this fixer-upper (me) was not very solid.

Chapter 2

Daddy Issues

Dad was always very athletic growing up. He didn't have an education because his parents made him quit school in sixth grade. My dad worked in the crop fields all year long to help support his family. Despite all this, he somehow managed to get into baseball and was even drafted to the minor league Dodgers. The major league came looking for him, but he was already working. He was such a great athlete that before my parents were married, he got the opportunity to carry the Olympic torch through California for the 1960 winter Olympics. Unfortunately, his career was short-lived after shattering his collarbone as he slid into 3rd base.

When Dad finally came back into our lives, he was married to Beatrice, who was ten years his senior. Even though mom allowed us to visit him, she still had her rules. One of which was that she did not want to see his new wife. For this reason, if my mom took us to dad's town, Tulare, he'd meet us at the A&W, but if he came to pick us up, we'd meet at the local gas station then pick up Bea around the corner.

Going on visits with dad was a special time for Tammy and me. We couldn't wait to be picked up but returning home was always awful. Saying mom despised my dad's new life would probably be an understatement. According to her, Beatrice was not our stepmom. We were never to see her as our stepmom, and we were never to call her our stepmom. And her four kids were most certainly not our step-brothers or sisters. It was such a sad situation. I loved Bea, but I could never say a word because I also loved mom and didn't want her to feel betrayed.

To make matters worse, Beatrice and my dad were Jehovah's Witness, which, for whatever reason, infuriated my mother. She made sure to let him know at every pickup and drop-off that Tammy and I were not Jehovah's Witnesses and he was not to take us along. No Kingdom Hall. No door knocking. Don't try to convert my daughters! We'd get home, and she'd start our interrogations, "Did they take you to Kingdom Hall?"

"Yes."

She calls him up and jumps all over his case about that.

"Did they take you door knocking?"

"Yes."

She calls him up and jumps all over his case about that.

Eventually, Tammy and I realized we'd just say "No" and keep the peace. Pretty sad when a child learns lying is the best route to keeping the peace. My dad never paid child support. And because he was Jehovah's Witness, we never received any presents from him for birthdays or Christmas. Well, I say never, but when Tammy turned eighteen, he bought her a necklace. I guess it was a 'just because you're an adult now' kind of thing. I'm not sure. All I know is I'm still waiting to receive the necklace he promised me.

Until the visitations with my dad began, my mom's mom was the only grandparent I knew. Then almost overnight, Tammy and I were introduced to two more grandmas and three more grandpas. My dad's parents were divorced, his mom had remarried, and then there were Bea's parents. All of which seemed to openly accept us into their lives without a second thought.

Whenever we went to visit my dad, he'd always take us to see his parents. First, we'd see Grandpa Mike. He would sit in his living room and roll his own cigarettes. His ring finger on his right hand was cut off at the knuckle, but he still wore a ring on that little nub. He'd hold his ZigZag paper right there on that little nub as he rolled his cigarettes. I didn't have the opportunity to get to know him because I didn't see my dad much. Grandpa died when I was 11, but I never went to his funeral because nobody told me he died. I didn't find out until a year later. It was a casual, "Oh, by the way, Grandpa Mike died last year."

What?

And life goes on. Tell me you wouldn't need therapy over that? I know it sounds like I'm joking, but man, it is crazy how such seemingly insignificant things bury down inside of us and change our whole perspective on how we see things.

After we visited Grandpa Mike, we'd go on to visit Grandma Petra and her husband, Rejino (I'm not fully confidant I spelled that correctly). She'd feed my dad, and then she'd feed us. I never had a chance to get close to her either because she didn't know a lick of English, and we didn't know any Spanish. We'd go there, we'd eat, and we'd leave unless my dad's sister Mary was there with her children. Then we'd spend some time playing with our cousins before we left. That was the extent of our visit.

It's no surprise that I became much closer with Beatrice's parents: Grandma Florence and Grandpa Weezer. Grandpa Weezer was my first real grandpa, even though he wasn't blood. We'd go out to their house in the country and run all over their property. We had so many fun adventures. When they sold that house and moved into town, they were close enough for me and Tammy to ride our bikes to their home for visits. We'd ride over there and spend time with them. It didn't matter if we were eating or just sitting around talking. Their house was always a nice escape from the craziness of our home.

Of course, my mom hated us calling Florence "Grandma," which made me do it all the more. I loved her just as much as my mom's mom. Why was loving somebody so wrong in her eyes? I shouldn't love Beatrice. I shouldn't love Grandma Florence, yet that was precisely what we were learning at this new church, to love one another. The confusion only thickened.

Unfortunately, all good things eventually come to an end. As I mentioned earlier, Beatrice was quite a bit older than my dad. She also had diabetes. One time, Bea got sick and had to be hospitalized. During this time, my dad was told she would soon die. Surprisingly, my mom took Tammy and me to the hospital to see her before she passed away. During that visit, my mom took a moment alone with Beatrice, and they forgave each other for all the hurtful things that were said between them.

Nobody had ever spoken to me about death. Beatrice's death was my first experience with losing a family member. That was when I was 11 years old. After Beatrice died, Tammy and I still rode our bikes to visit Grandma Florence and Grandpa Weezer until Grandma Florence passed away the following year.

It wasn't until after Beatrice died that we learned my dad had an affair and was no longer with Beatrice. They didn't want us to know. Beatrice probably knew we didn't need any more complications in our young lives. He had cheated on her while she was in the hospital. This choice had him exiled from the Jehovah's Witness. Dad finally had a son, and he named him after himself, Valentino, or Tin [pronounced 'teen'] for short. Once Tin was born, I stopped calling him daddy. I was so upset about what he had done to Bea that I just called him dad.

Once again, the building materials were not the greatest. My daddy issues led to Father issues when I became a Christian. A Heavenly Father sounded a little far-fetched and maybe too good to be true. It was mostly in part to my dad's many broken promises that I soon began believing, "Promises were meant to be broken." As I grew up, it became one of my life quotes.

It was also a hindrance when, as an adult, I became a new believer and was told the many promises of the Bible. I had a hard time believing any of those promises were for me. I thought they were for everyone else. No one ever kept their promises to me. So, naturally, I thought, why should God apply His promises to me? Who was I to deserve them? He didn't owe me anything, so there was no point in believing they were relevant to me.

I remember mentioning this to my mom after I had become a Christian, and she said, "The devil is a liar! Those promises are for you."

It was wonderful to hear this coming from my mom. However, accepting those promises for myself would take some reprogramming. I would have to allow God to dig out all the lies that had taken root in my life. "Promises were meant to be broken." This wasn't a one-time event in my life but rather a repeat offender, something that I'd have to roll up my sleeves and work at little by little until it no longer had a place in my heart.

> *"Let your roots grow down into him, and let your lives be built on him. Then your faith will grow strong in the truth you were taught, and you will overflow with thankfulness. Don't let anyone capture you with empty philosophies and high-sounding nonsense that come from human thinking and from the spiritual powers of this world, rather than from Christ." Colossians 2:7&8 NLT*

If we can have roots that grow down deep in Christ, isn't it understood that we could also have roots that grow down deep in the world? 'Promises were meant to be broken' was a lie that took root in my life. 'Relationships were not meant to last,' 'Mothers and daughters were meant to have conflict,' 'I wasn't into girlie stuff, so maybe I couldn't be girlie.' All these lies began growing down into my life and taking root at such a young age. As we continue on this journey, you'll see how some of them grew wildly out of control.

Losing Bea was heartbreaking. But nothing was as painful as my dad's betrayal of Bea. I loved her so much. How could he do such a thing? I hated him for what he had done.

> *"Most important of all, continue to show deep love*
> *for each other, for love covers a multitude of sins."*
> *1 Peter 4:8 NLT*

As I mentioned throughout the chapter, my mom had quite the distaste for Bea. She allowed bitterness and jealousy to drive her actions towards Bea, her children, or her parents. Thankfully, she came around, and they made their peace with one another in the end. But I wonder how much different the story I'm writing would be if everyone had allowed themselves to *"show deep love for each other."*

Chapter 3

Tainted Religion

It was during third grade when my mom brought home Luis. He was an okay guy. I mean, he had fuzzy hair and a shaggy beard. He had one cross-eye and a bar of silver that capped one front tooth. Okay, looking back, he could have easily been cast as a creepy kidnapper in a movie. He didn't speak much English at all, which meant he'd only converse with my mom. I don't remember much about him in the early days, just that he showed up one day and never left.

Before Luis showed up, we were practicing Catholics. Catholicism was something my Grandma passed down to my mom. She was a diehard Catholic. Every Saturday, mom would take us to Catechism. We never went to mass on Sundays, like Grandma, but we would attend mass for special occasions such as weddings, funerals, and maybe Christmas. I made my First Holy Communion that year, and the next thing I knew, I found myself at the First Assemblies of God. It was like one weekend we were Catholic, and the next we were Pentecostal. But do you think anyone bothered to tell us why we suddenly switched religions? No. We were just kids. Why did we need to know any details? The conversion was one more stake between my

Grandma and mom's relationship. And for what? Why had she suddenly converted?

It wasn't until my teen years that I discovered the reason for the sudden conversion. My mom and Luis were driving down this two-lane country road around ten o'clock at night, surrounded by vineyards, when this woman appeared out of nowhere. My mom described it as if she'd been thrown into the car. The woman was killed instantly, but because this was before cellphones, they had to drive ten miles to reach the nearest house and call the police.

This action added a 'hit and run' charge to the manslaughter charge. Since Luis was an illegal alien and he was driving, he convinced my mom to take the wrap. So, what does she do? My mom took the wrap because she didn't want to see him deported. Mom went to trial, and although she was found not guilty, the stress caused by the whole ordeal led her to our conversion. The Catholic church hadn't offered her any comfort during this ordeal, so she turned to the Assemblies of God church. That is when she got saved and became a full-fledge Jesus freak with a lot of legalism. I'm pretty sure the legalism was mostly in part to the Catholic rituals ingrained in her upbringing. From what I could tell, she simply moved her membership.

Catholic or Assemblies, it made no difference to me. I loved going to church when I was younger. Mom took us to Sunday school, children's church, and Missionettes. I really liked our new church family and the activities we were involved in throughout the week.

As you'll read about later in the book, my love for church attendance began to fade. I believe it was mainly due to my mom's hypocritical lifestyle. She'd go to church and be a 'Christian'; then she would come home and shack up with Luis. There was no life-altering conversion of her heart from what I could see. Because of these double standards, I soon began to think of all Christians as hypocrites.

Now, I'm sure some of you might think, "Wow, Priscilla, you're really hard on your mom. You must have an awful relationship with her." That couldn't be further from the truth. Remember that attached kindergartener? My mother and I were super close and still are. However, that doesn't mean we haven't gone through moments where we simply didn't see eye to eye or maybe even couldn't stand each other from time to time. Just because you don't like something, someone doesn't necessarily mean you stop loving that person, especially your mom.

When I refer to my mom and her religion, it is through the lens of what is spoken in *Matthew 16:24, "Then Jesus said to his disciples, "If any of you wants to be my follower, you must give up your own way, take up your cross, and follow me."*

When there is still so much of our own way running havoc in our life, it is hard for observers to associate us as one of Christ's followers.

Another scripture that comes to mind is *Matthew 7:1-5, "Do not judge others, and you will not be judged. For you will be treated as you treat others. The standard you use in judging is the standard by which you will be judged. And why worry about a speck in your friend's eye when you have a log in your own? How can you think of saying to your friend, 'Let me help you get rid of that speck in your eye,' when you can't see past the log in your own eye? Hypocrite! First get rid of the log in your own eye; then you will see well enough to deal with the speck in your friend's eye."*

Do you know what Jesus was saying? We can't try to help someone else with their sin if we've never taken the time to deal with our own sin. I made many bad decisions, and mom always seemed to be quick to point them out. I always took this as judgment and never instruction for self-improvement. Why? Tone and context.

She was never loving when she addressed the matter; instead, she was continually telling me I was going to hell for my choices, my sins. On top of that, all the while she is telling me to deal with my sin and get rid of my sin, she herself is strutting her sin like a model on a catwalk.

Was she perfect? No. Was I perfect? No. Am I perfect now? Still no. But all the while, she has been my mother, and I still love her to this day. I am openly honest about all of this, not so you will form an opinion one way or another about my mother, but so you can have a vivid picture of the confusion, and division hypocrisy can cause.

> *"But don't just listen to God's word. You must do what it says. Otherwise, you are only fooling yourselves. For if you listen to the word and don't obey, it is like glancing at your face in a mirror. You see yourself, walk away, and forget what you look like. But if you look carefully into the perfect law that sets you free, and if you do what it says and don't forget what you heard, then God will bless you for doing it." James 1:22-25 NLT*

Live for God, or don't, but never choose to teeter-totter between the two. It will only cause pain for you and all those who observe you.

Chapter 4

The Nightmares

When I was ten, my sister Tammy and I were already asleep in bed; we had slept with each other our entire lives. Even though we now had our own room, we still wanted to sleep together, so; we would push our twin beds together. One evening, I woke up because I felt something, or rather someone's presence. As I slowly opened my eyes, I saw an arm coming through the window, heading towards my sister's crotch. I sat up in the dark but was unable to scream. I tried so hard, but I was scared frozen. My mouth was moving, but nothing was coming out, then suddenly, I mustered up the loudest scream. The arm jerked out the window.

Tammy sat up straight, and my mom came running into the room. I was so scared that when my mom entered the room, all I could say was, "the arm, the arm." The window was still open enough for my mom to see it was not a dream. She called 911 and told them we had an intruder on our property.

Minutes later, Luis walks into the house. He had been drinking, as usual. Mom began telling him what happened, and then I saw the bracelet on his arm. It was the same as the arm that had come through the window. I yelled, "It was him! It was him."

Luis spoke very broken English, and since we didn't speak Spanish, I had no idea what he told my mom. But right before the police came, mom told us not to say a word. When they did arrive, mom did all the talking with Luis right by her side. The female police officer knelt in front of me and asked me if I remembered anything about the incident. I looked at my mom. She gave me the 'mom look'; you know that one that says you better do exactly as you had been told and keep your mouth shut.

I replied, "No."

The police officer looked at my mom then back to me. "Are you sure?" I think she suspected I knew something more.

"Yes," I replied. Once again, lying to keep the peace.

Several weeks later, he tried to molest my sister again. She told mom, but mom never did anything about it. She and Luis would fight, always in Spanish, but he never left. And now, since Tammy was vocal about it, he never touched her again. So, I was next in line. At first, he started by playing and tickling me. He'd take me to the store and make me feel special. Slowly he began to get closer to my private areas. When he would get closer, I would freeze. I was only ten, I wasn't sure what was happening, but I knew it wasn't right in my gut. Eventually, he started to grope me. I began to push him away. Then there was one time I got bold enough to say, "If you don't stop, I'm going to tell my mom."

He told me if I told anyone, my mom would go to jail. At that time, my little brain correlated the cops being there the first time, and nothing happens to him. Since my mom didn't say anything at the time and told us not to say anything, maybe he was right. Perhaps she would get in trouble if I said something. I didn't want to see my mom go to jail. Like I mentioned earlier, I was attached to my mom's hip. Thinking that I could lose her was enough to keep me silent.

As months went on, the molestation increased to daily, nightly, and whenever else he could get his grubby hands on me. I couldn't even walk down the hall without getting groped. There came the point when he started to throw me up in the attic to have his way with me. I became a reader. At night, I would tuck myself way back in the furthest corner of the closet with a flashlight and read until I knew he was no longer a threat. I would hear him come into my room, but he would not risk looking for me, knowing he could wake up my sister. I did not always escape him. Mom would often send me to the store with him; I would clutch onto the door handle with both hands every time.

Not only did I have to have a hiding place at night, but I also had to have a hiding place in the daytime if my mom wasn't home. My favorite place was on the roof of the house. I loved to sit up there and watch Luis as he looked for me. Other times I would climb the tree in the front yard, and he would beg for me to come down, promising me this or that. The saddest place I would hide is under the freeway bridge that was adjacent to our house. At the very top, on a ledge, is where I would sit and wait for my mom to get home. I could feel the vibration of the cars as they drove over my head. During those moments, I would wish he would die or just go away.

There were three occasions when Luis scared me more than I had ever been scared before as a child. And it was in two of those times that he completely stole my innocence.

I was a die-hard Charlie's Angels fan back in 1976, and I used to stay up late because it would air at 10 PM. Usually, mom would stay up to watch it with me or one of my other siblings. But on this particular night, I was alone. Halfway through the show, Luis came home drunk. I should have turned off the TV and ran to my room, but I didn't. Instead, I sat frozen, hoping he'd ignore me. Unfortunately for me, he sat next to me on the couch. There was a struggle, and I tried not to scream. He eventually penetrated me with his fingers. I jumped off the couch very quickly and ran to my room. It was on that night I had decided there was no God. This God that my mom always talked about watching over me? No, He most certainly wasn't. He was nowhere to be found. I cried in fear, not knowing for sure what Luis had done to me. All I knew is it felt wrong, and I never wanted it to happen again.

Another time we took a trip to Los Angeles. Since Porterville was a small country town tucked in the middle of the San Joaquin Valley, it was my first-time seeing city lights. Luis had a 1970's van with the triangle bubble windows in the back. I was kneeling between the two fronts seats, amazed at the city lights and the tall buildings, when he reached back and stuck his hand down my pants. I cringed and then bit his arm super hard. He shouted and pulled his hand out. My mom asked him what had happened, and he told her I bit him. She asked me why I would do such a thing, but all I could think about was her going to jail if I told the truth, so I replied, "I don't know."

On the third occasion, I had been swimming at the city pool. It was the place all the kids would go to during the summer. I had on this tiny yellow bikini. I was a skinny, scrawny bean pole of a kid; probably why my uncle gave me the nickname "Slinky Linky." When I got home, I had a terrible rolling leg cramp that my mom could not get to go away. It was a horrible Charlie horse rolling down my leg. Mom decided she needed to get Bengay to put on my leg. So, she left and headed to Thirty's Drug Store. The only people left in the house were me, Mike, Mark, and Luis. I was maybe, ten. I was lying on the bed, and Luis came into the room and shut the door. As I was lying there with this awful leg cramp, he began to molest me. I was trying to get away from him, but he laid on top of me and unzipped his pants. In my little brain, I knew something worse than I had ever experienced was about to happen to me.

I began screaming for my brothers, who were only seven at the time, to open the door. Luis was screaming at them, telling them not to open the door or they were going to get it. Since this was an older house, it had those old metal doorknobs, and some of the doorknobs were missing, so you had to use the end of a fork or spoon to turn the latch. I could hear my brothers just outside the door struggling to get the door open and dropping the fork or spoon they were using and screaming in fear that they were trying.

When that door swung open, it was like the moment you burst through the surface of water when you think you might be drowning. Luis immediately moved to the side of me, and I ran out of the room. He yelled at us to shut the door as he laid face down on the bed, but we refused. He squirmed to the edge of the bed and slammed the door shut. I looked at my panicked brothers and told them I was ok. Then I told them not to say anything to mom. And when mom got home, we never said a word.

"Jesus said to the people who believed in him, "You are truly my disciples if you remain faithful to my teachings. And you will know the truth, and the truth will set you free.

"But we are descendants of Abraham," they said. "We have never been slaves to anyone. What do you mean, 'You will be set free'?"

Jesus replied, "I tell you the truth, everyone who sins is a slave of sin. A slave is not a permanent member of the family, but a son is part of the family forever. So if the Son sets you free, you are truly free." John 8:31-35

It was a lie that started my nightmares. It quenched my boldness and kept me quiet. "If you say anything, your mom will go to jail." There was no truth in this statement, but how could I know this?

Luis would tell me horrible, awful things during this time of my life. Things like, "One day, you'll appreciate what I'm doing." Or, "You know you like what I am doing to you; I know it feels good." All twisted, awful lies from the pit of hell.

There was undoubtedly physical abuse, but the verbal and psychological abuse left far more devastation in my life. They drug me into an ongoing cycle of confusion, fear, hate, shame, and guilt. I would find this cycle continuing throughout my teen years and into my adult life.

Chapter 5

The Confusion

I was pretty smart in school. But the abuse got worse and increased to the point that I began to withdraw. I was uncomfortable all the time at home. I couldn't walk down the hallway without him groping me, grabbing me, or sticking his tongue in my mouth. I would beg my mom to let me go live with my aunt or anybody else. She didn't understand. How could she? I never told her what was happening. I couldn't, not if I wanted to protect her.

My mom got pregnant, and along came my little brother Louie. He was named after his father, Luis. Mom was still taking us to church during this time and telling us all the things that are right and wrong while she's shacking up with Luis, who is sexually abusing me and having a child out of wedlock. If that doesn't cause confusion, I'm not sure what would.

In the middle of my sixth-grade school year, my mom sent me to live with my aunt and uncle and my cousin Isaac, the same cousin from my kindergarten class. We had always been close friends and finally life was good again. Since Luis was no longer around, I didn't have to be on guard. I was finally able to relax and be a kid again. I was safe.

My mom must have seen a change in me because she came knocking on the door to take me home a few months later. Something made her decide the problem must have been at my school. After all, I was doing fine at Isaac's school, so why not drag me back home. She used a friend's address to enroll me in another school across town. Since it was out of our school district, mom had Luis drive me to school. I hated those days. I'd sit holding the door handle, ready to jump out the door if he reached for me. It's unfortunate looking back and seeing how she made these decisions, thinking it was helping but all the while making things worse. I enjoyed my class before I moved to my aunt's house. And, of course, I loved living at my aunt's house. But for whatever reason, here I was at my third school for my sixth-grade school year.

There were times I would stay with her friend's family during the week. Although I felt like the outcast of the family, I was thankful for those days because Luis wouldn't be driving me to school. The shuffling from house to house left me feeling very isolated and alone. It was during this time I learned how to numb out. I used this method to detach myself from the abuse. There was no point in crying because that never made it go away.

This feeling of being isolated and alone was something I carried on into adulthood. It's not a conclusion I came to on my own but eventually discovered through a good counselor's help.

I'm sure it was during this time that the idea, "I'm young, I'll bounce back." most likely began taking shape in my mind. It was a thought that eventually became a life motto. Whenever bad things happened, I'd simply tell myself, "I'm young, I'll bounce back."

To further add to all the confusion of my life, when I turned twelve and started seventh grade, Luis's abuse stopped.

No explanation, no here or there. It merely stopped altogether. When I got older, I became more open about the abuse I had endured. Sometime last year, a friend of mine, a retired vice cop who dealt with crimes against children, told me the abuse had most likely stopped because I had reached a point where I was beyond his desirable age. I never realized that molesters had specific age ranges they targeted.

Although the abuse had stopped and I hadn't done anything wrong, I still felt disgusting, dirty, and worthless from all that had transpired. Not to mention the awful outlook I had towards men. The shuffling from place to place, the displacement from my family, the sexual abuse- all these things had laid the foundation of confusion in my life.

> *"If the godly give in to the wicked, it's like polluting a fountain or muddying a spring."*
> *Proverbs 25:26 NLT*

That is precisely how I would describe my life as I'm looking back on it. A muddy pool of water. Have you ever been to a lake or the ocean and you can't see the bottom? Then you step on something squishy. Immediately trust, and confidence goes away, so you either proceed cautiously or just get out.

I could not trust my mom and could not trust God. Once again, alone.

Chapter 6

Let Me Tell You 'Bout My Best Friend

W ho was your first best friend in elementary school? I bet their name immediately popped into your head when I asked the question. You remember those good times and maybe even a few rough moments. Mine was Sheila Patrick. We met in third grade. Just to set the stage, our whole neighborhood was full of Hispanic families. Then here comes Sheila's mom, Pat, with her five daughters. They were the whitest white people I knew. I say that with all the love in my heart. We were from two different cultural backgrounds. We were Hispanic; we ate everything with tortillas using our fingers. And we certainly had never tried this 'chicken and dumplings' stuff that Pat made. It was amazing!

The first time we met Pat's three youngest girls, they sat outside their house on the curb looking really sad. Sheila was playing with ants, poking them with a stick. I learned later that they had moved from Northern California, so I imagine they were feeling pretty lost at that moment. Tammy and I walked across the street, introduced ourselves, and that became the start of a beautiful friendship. Sheila's sister, Verlene was the same age as Tammy, her younger sister, Darlene, was the same age as the twins, and Sheila was the same age as me. It couldn't have been more perfect.

Sheila's mom was also divorced. I'm not sure if she worked because I only remember her always sitting on the couch watching soap operas, drinking coffee, and smoking cigarettes. Since Sheila's dad didn't pay child support either, I'm assuming her mom depended on welfare and food stamps as we did, but I don't know.

Oh, food stamps! I remember getting government cheese, government butter, and government powder milk (just add water)- yuck! But because food stamps were only on the first of the month, we would run out of food before the month ended. One time, we sat in a circle in the middle of the living room and ate oranges for dinner. Free school lunches were the healthiest meal of the day. We didn't think anything of it. When your best friend lives a similar life, it's easy to mark that as the standard for normal.

Looking back, I can see how we were poor at the time. I never cared. I never noticed. Summer vacations? What were those? We never went on vacation. We couldn't afford stuff like that. Our summer break from school consisted of running through the school's sprinkler system and playing on the jungle gym. We'd do other outdoor activities such as hopscotch, jacks, and Chinese jump rope. After school and during the summer, we'd pretty much run the neighborhood until the streetlights came on. Were we lacking? If we were, every other kid in our neighborhood was lacking, so we never noticed.

Pat was a lot less strict than my mom. Sheila and her sisters would continue running the neighborhood even after dark; there were weeks when Sheila would stay over five nights in a row before Pat would finally make her go home. She was the very best friend anyone could ask for during those early years.

"There are "friends" who destroy each other, but a real friend sticks closer than a brother."
Proverbs 18:24 NLT

Sheila was my 'real' friend throughout grade school. She was the one who stuck closer to me than anyone else. She made her mark on my life as I'm sure I did on hers. I have so many stories of our time together, but that would have to be a whole other book.

I still remember the summer after 8th grade when Sheila came to my house, with big tears in her eyes, and told me her mom was moving them all back to Chico, California. We all cried. I lost my best friend. True friends might come and go, but they never leave your life. Thankfully, I was able to reconnect with Sheila through the wonderful world of social media later on in my adult years. It's interesting how best friends can get back together after so many years apart and just click all over again.

Chapter 7

The Seed of Rebellion

Up to seventh grade, I would say I was a pretty good child. Even though I didn't understand the hypocrisy I often witnessed with religion, I had a vague respect, or fear, of God, or maybe it was hell. Even with all I had been through, my moral compass still had some decent direction in it. However, this is where things begin to turn a little darker.

There was a time when my dad and Beatrice took Tammy and me to Disneyland. While we were standing in line to buy tickets, I noticed a group of kids acting up. I could tell they were there without any supervision because they were acting a bit wild. There was something about them that immediately attracted me. I was this meek little girl full of guilt and shame, but these kids- they had power. I wanted the same kind of power. I wanted that same freedom. It was in that moment the spirit of rebellion drew me in hook, line, and sinker. It was such a tiny seed planted in my little heart, and it stayed buried until that transition between sixth and seventh grade. It was then that the tiny seed of rebellion decided to sprout up.

It started with the simplest of things. Sheila had some pot and asked if I wanted to smoke it. At first, I was mortified. All the condemning church talks about sins led me to believe I could probably go to hell just for looking at the pot. But for whatever reason, at that moment, I thought about those rebellious kids at Disneyland. Those unruly kids with so much power, not answering to no one. "Let's do it!"

We smoked that pot, and I felt like I was in heaven. I had chosen for myself, which made me feel like I had obtained some power over my life. I was going against my mother, the one who constantly nagged me for everything I was doing wrong but never knew all that I was enduring in her house; that also felt good. But, the best feeling of all was when the pot numbed me out more than shutting myself down. I didn't have a care in the world. I didn't have to worry about who I was or what had happened to me. I was free of my home life. That's when I decided these big bad kids in junior high were the ones I wanted to hang out with permanently. They attracted me like a moth to a flame, just like those Disneyland kids. I was introduced to other things, like sniffing glue and paint. At first, my innocent church girl came out, and I thought it was something really wrong. But the more I hung around with my new friends and the more we did it, the less wrong it became.

Although my mom had never really worked much in the past, I remember her working nights during this time. Luis would come home drunk and start arguments with me and my sister Tammy. By this time, we were a bit older, and for me, because the abuse had stopped, just a little braver, I started calling him names and talking back, even throwing out the occasional F-bomb.

Then one night, I woke up and walked through the house. I'm not quite sure why; maybe I was getting a drink of water or going to the bathroom. All I know is I walked by the living room and saw Luis passed out drunk on the living room floor. No surprise there. But what *was* surprising was that he was completely naked! I ran to the room and woke up Sheila and Tammy. "Luis is lying naked on the floor."

Of course, they didn't believe me, so they quietly snuck out to the living room with me. None of us had seen a naked man before, so we're grossed out and giggling at the same time.

"I'm calling Mom," Tammy said, and that's precisely what she did.

My mom came home and found Luis still passed out on the floor, still naked. There was yelling, there was screaming, nothing new. But this time, he swung back his fist and punched her right in the face. Something snapped in the three of us girls because the very next minute, all three of us jumped on him and started punching him.

"You, bitches, get off me!" he yelled as he tried getting away.

I grabbed a handful of his chest hair and ripped it right out. Man, that was an incredible feeling. He finally managed to get to the front porch. At that point, he got us off of him and left. It was such a victorious night. He was gone! But the victory didn't last long; he eventually came back because she always let him.

"And now, dear brothers and sisters, one final thing. Fix your thoughts on what is true, and honorable, and right, and pure, and lovely, and admirable. Think about things that are excellent and worthy of praise." Philippians 4:8

Those kids at Disneyland were just the first example of a thought that lingered until it became a reality. I hadn't read the Bible, so I had no Biblical knowledge. I had no idea what I should and shouldn't be filling my mind with; it's those seeds that sprout roots.

Chapter 8

Mike Madrid

Seventh grade was also the time I had my first crush. It was an unbelievable crush on a boy named Mike Madrid. But I was afraid because he was a boy. My only experience with a male person was Luis's abuse, so I wasn't sure what to expect.

Around that time, I was in a *quinceanera*. If you're not familiar with this, it is a Hispanic ritual similar to a sweet sixteen party. In Hispanic culture, the young girl turning 15 has 14 other girls representing her at the party. They are called *damas*. Each of these girls represents a year of her life. All fourteen walk down the aisle at the Catholic church, similar to a wedding but without a groom. Then she walks in as the fifteenth girl since it is her 15th birthday. I had to wear a dress and look like a frilly girlie girl. Ugh! I was out of my comfort zone and so nervous the whole day. Each of the *damas* walks into the room partnered with a young man. I had asked Mike Madrid to be my partner. That made the frilly dress somewhat worth it.

Later that night, they had a reception. That's when they brought out the champagne. He grabbed a bottle like it was nothing, and we started drinking. Here I am, yet again, with another first, that shouldn't be bestowed upon someone my age. At thirteen years old, I experienced my first alcoholic buzz.

What does alcohol do for you? It changes you into somebody new. Alcohol was even better than the numbing feeling of pot. Now I could speak to Mike Madrid, and no nerves were holding me back. It instantly gave me everything I sought. I wasn't a meek, insecure, helpless, broken child. In my mind, I now had some courage. I could dance and socialize. I found myself bold enough to receive my first boy/girl kiss from Mike Madrid. I even found myself somewhere outside the party making out with him. All my fears of guys had suddenly been buzzed away with the alcohol, and it was all good.

After the party, he called me and asked me to meet him at the park. I was head over heels for that guy. Unfortunately, he never showed up, so I went home heartbroken and depressed. The first guy I had let my guard down to, and he stood me up? My sister Tammy had so much compassion for me. She played the song "Sitting in the Park" by Billy Stewart. As you can probably guess, every time I hear that song, I think of him, even to this day. When we spoke at school, I discovered that he, too, thought he'd been stood up. It was just a mix-up; we had gone to separate parks. I still had a crush on him, but nothing went any further.

And during the following summer, he began dating a girl named Sarah just like the Fleetwood Mac song that had been released that same year and played everywhere. Man, I hated that song! I couldn't stand it! I saw them walking in the halls together, going to class; it made me jealous.

I'm sure I told mom about it at some point, but she had no sympathy for my loss. She didn't want me to have anything to do with that ungodly, unholy thing. All I could think was, *You are such a hypocrite. You're sleeping with this man who is not your husband. This man who has molested me, and you're telling me someone else is ungodly?* That is where I learned to hate Christians. Her hypocrisy fueled me.

"Don't be drunk with wine, because that will ruin your life. Instead, be filled with the Holy Spirit, singing psalms and hymns and spiritual songs among yourselves, and making music to the Lord in your hearts." Ephesians 5:18&19 NLT

Man, I wish I could go back and tell my thirteen-year-old self the words from this scripture. Thirteen and already, I had lived through so much trauma, confusion, and pain. I don't blame younger me for wanting to numb out. I didn't have anyone I could trust with all that I was going through. It was easier to accept the high or accept the numbing feeling and allow those things to help me deal with life.

Chapter 9

Desires of the Heart

In Porterville, when I was growing up, we had two ethnic groups. You were either Mexican or white. Sheila and I hung out with the Mexican kids, and my sister hung out with the white kids. In those days, a lot of the Mexican kids were Cholos or Cholas. They wore khakis and drove low riders. The Cholos were known for being associated with gangs. Mike Madrid was one of them, and that made it that much more appealing.

I started dressing like them, which made my mom furious. She refused to buy me khakis or Dickey pants. So, I asked my Aunt Lupe if she would get me some school clothes. She did, which made my mother even more upset. I was hanging out with all these kids, and my mom was livid; I'm pretty sure she was about to disown me. She would say, "Tell me who you hang out with, and I'll tell you who you are." I didn't really care. These were my friends; they accepted me. Since this was right around the time Sheila moved, it made me dive into these relationships that much more.

Around this time, I experienced my first anxiety attack. My heart was beating so fast I thought I was going to die. I woke up my mom, telling her I couldn't breathe. I didn't know what it was, and she didn't know what it was, so she called an ambulance. They took me away and kept me for a little while. They told her there was nothing wrong and sent me home. Back then, they didn't talk a lot about anxiety, and no one dared to consider PTSD. If they had questioned me, it would have been obvious. I was experiencing PTSD from my encounters with Luis, which were causing the anxiety attacks.

Because they became persistent and I was always in the hospital, they sent me to a cardiologist. He decided I should wear a heart monitor for 24 hours. I had always loved sports and was very active in track and field, softball, and basketball. Regrettably, the school decided that I could be a potential liability because of the heart monitor, and they required me to withdraw from all sports. I was never allowed to play sports again after that. Just one more thing I lost of myself.

That same year, I met Yolanda and Katrina. They were from homes where their parents didn't keep them in check. I became really good friends with Katrina, and I hung out with her so often that I became close to her family. She had a brother named John and an older sister named Anna. Katrina invited me to spend the night all the time, and I would as often as my mom would let me.

Anna was a Chola, and she was as butch as they come. So much so that I thought she was Katrina's older brother when I first met her. Up to this point in my life, I had never had any encounters with lesbians or gays. I'm not even sure I knew they existed until I met Anna. All I knew was that she looked so mean the first time I met her. She walked into the house, and my eyes grew huge. She looked straight at me and said, "What the f- are you looking at, punk?"

I quickly replied. "Nothing."

She laughed so hard because she knew she had scared me.

By this time, I had also experienced making out with boys. Because of my abuse and the damage done to my psyche, I was gripped continuously with fear no matter who the boy was. It would start as something I wanted to do, but the moment they would touch me or grope me, I'd be fearful of saying no. Afraid of what might happen to me if I did say no. So, I'd let them do what they wanted but never took it as far as sex. It was a very uncomfortable experience. I'm sure it had some contributions to my constant chest pains and anxiety attacks.

At the same time, I began fantasizing about what it might be like to kiss a girl. The thought first crossed my mind regarding my friend Yolanda. It was an innocent thought that popped into my head out of nowhere. At first, I thought, "Well, that was weird. Why'd I think about that?"

My mom decided to end things with Luis once again. Only this time, she decided she wanted to move thirty minutes away. That meant I'd have to switch schools again! I told her I didn't want to go, and for some reason, she didn't make me. Instead, she allowed me to live with Katrina's family. They were happy to take me in. She took all my siblings and left me there in Porterville.

I'm sure I missed Tammy and my siblings, but life was great. Katrina's mom was cool. She didn't hover around asking a bunch of questions or interrogated us over every decision. She let us smoke pot. Living in this home is what my rebellious teenage heart wanted but had no business being around.

Katrina's parents had their own cleaning business and would often be out cleaning office buildings at night which meant we were left to do as we pleased, which is why I ended up having my first encounter with the police while I was living there. We vandalized the school and almost got caught. When the police questioned us about what we knew, I lied. They asked where my mom was, and I told them she was in Tulare. I was staying with the Garcias, and I didn't have anything else to say to them.

While I was living with them, Anna went to San Francisco and came back with some friends. They were all gay, every single one of them. Katrina's parents put a house on the back of their property to give Anna her own space since she was nineteen. She'd have parties with her friend, and we'd go back to join them.

I didn't have much of a thought about what it truly meant to be gay. It never even crossed my mind that hanging around Anna was probably what brought about the idea of kissing Yolanda. All I knew was these gay people knew how to party, and I liked it. I remember one of Anna's friends named "Teardrop". She stuck out to me because she was a girl but looked just like a guy. Seeing girls looking like guys had become such a normal thing to see every day. My mom was clueless that she had left me in this environment.

I loved living with Katrina's family, and my mom would call every once in a while to check on me. I'd always tell her everything was good. And life was *so* good until six months later when mom moved back. Once again, she decided to get back with Luis. Katrina and I stayed good friends until high school. When we reached high school, we went to separate schools and drifted apart from each other.

When mom came back, she threw a party for my 8th-grade graduation. It was a big party with many friends, and some of the guys started smoking pot. I don't know what happened, but Luis got his gun, pointed it at them, and told them to leave. He was drunk and started an embarrassing fiasco. He's screaming, mom's screaming, and all the guys are stoned. It was chaotic, and to me, this was a normal life.

"Temptation comes from our own desires, which entice us and drag us away. These desires give birth to sinful actions. And when sin is allowed to grow, it gives birth to death." James 1:14&15 NLT

Back then, I didn't realize the power one thought could have on my life. Rather than dismiss it, I decided to let it linger. And linger around it did until it became more and more present. I had no idea things were happening all around me in the spirit realm. No idea that hanging around Anna and her friends was opening a door for me to become familiar and comfortable with a spirit of homosexuality. Hanging around her was probably also the reason I began fantasizing about kissing a female. My mom was right when she said, "Show me your friends, and I'll show you who you are."

Chapter 10

You Only Live Once

I'm not sure how high school works nowadays, but back then, in our town, we had four categories of students divided into. There was the SOC [pronounced so-sh]. They were the kids living the social life- the jocks, cheerleaders, ones with money. Then there were the stoners. Aside from those two, you had the Hispanic kids who identified as Cholos or Cholas and the white kids who identified as rednecks. SOC, Cholos, stoners, and rednecks- that was how the world worked back then in Porterville.

My sister Tammy was a SOC. Even though she came from a poor Hispanic family, she worked her butt off so she could wear those fancy clothes. And yes, she was even a cheerleader. She walked the walk and talked the talk so well that no one ever suspected she was from the same welfare family as I was. Actually, most people didn't even know we were related. Which is kind of comical since nowadays people tell us how much we look alike.

Unlike Miss Goody Two-Shoes Tammy, I hung out with the Cholos. I smoked pot, drank, and cussed. She was mama's good girl, and I was the one mom fought on everything. I started ninth grade with the big bad Mexicans. I hung out with people who were older than me- juniors and seniors.

It's my freshman year in high school, and of course, we moved AGAIN—this time to the other side of town. I would like to say it's without Luis, but that would have been too good to be true.

By this point, Mike Madrid had broken up with Sarah (woohoo!). Unfortunately, he had also moved to another town which meant we'd no longer have any classes together. Two weeks before December, I saw him outside his old house. I think they were trying to sell it or something. We started talking about his new school and some other stuff. After our goodbyes, I started walking back to the high school, which was across the street. I was halfway across the street when he yelled out, "Priscilla,"

I stopped in the middle of the street and looked back at him. He looked at me for a moment and added, "take care."

Man, I wish he didn't have to move and go to another school. Mike was a good friend. "You too!" I replied and headed into the school.

When I got to school on December 2, 1980 my friend asked if I had heard about Mike Madrid.

I said, "Heard what?"

My friend replied, "He was stabbed last night at the Visalia Christmas Parade and was killed."

I couldn't believe what I was hearing. Mike Madrid, dead? But I had just seen him two weeks ago. I put my books in my locker and cried as I walked home. When I got home, my mom asked what I was doing home from school. I told her Mike Madrid had died and I couldn't be there.

She said, "Why do you care? He came from a bad family."

That's calling the kettle black

I went to my room, cried, and numbed out.

By this time in my life, my mom was now dragging me to church with hangovers. Her saying was, "If you can stay out all night partying, you can go to church."

My mom's response to Mike Madrid's death hit me so hard that I never bothered to take the time to grieve. I went to the funeral with Katrina and her family. It was the hardest day of my life. I watched as they lowered the casket into the ground. The casket of a teenage boy who was 15 years old. A boy who had been my first crush. He wasn't supposed to be dead yet; that's not how it was supposed to work.

I stood by that casket until they put the last bit of dirt on him. Then Katrina and I went to her aunt's house. She was a drunk, so we all got hammered drunk. That night, another truth was solidified inside of me that would follow me into adulthood. If you don't want to feel anything, you drown it out. Because when you drink, it all goes away, and you don't have to deal with it. Not the death of your friend, not the lack of empathy from your mother, none of it. The alcohol drowns it all out, and you don't feel a thing.

Except empty.

Chapter 11

Mija, Don't Do That!

After the summer of my freshman year, I got a job at Golden Corral. That is where I met Jana. Jana was white. But unlike Sheila, who was now more Hispanic than me, Jana was in the redneck group. She was in Future Farmers of America and wore Wrangler jeans. We were like night and day. Since many of my other friends were older and had graduated this past year, I began spending the summer with Jana. We hung out a lot, and she told me I needed to stop wearing Dickies and Khakis. I liked Jana; she wasn't like my other friends. She was innocent. I suppose that is why I went along with the idea of her taking me school shopping at the Wrangler Store. I ended up coming home with some Wrangler jeans and a belt that had my name on the back of it. My mom was super excited. Jana was a good influence on me.

I, on the other hand, was an awful influence on Jana. Her parents sheltered her quite a bit. I introduced her to alcohol, specifically vodka, and her mother hated me. We hung around her redneck friends that summer, and they became my red-neck friends. So, when I started my 10th-grade year, there was a whole new kind of struggle. I had been a Pendleton khaki wearing Hispanic, and now I was a redneck. To all my previous friends, I was a traitor- a f'ing coconut. I was brown on the outside but acting like I was white on the inside.

Because I had such a transformation in how I dressed, many teachers didn't remember me from the previous year. They treated me differently as a 'coconut' than they did when I was a Mexican. Now, I'm hanging with the white kids in Wrangler jeans. I no longer *looked* like I would give them any problems, but I did just in a different way. My overall school record would say otherwise, but I could tell there was a difference. As an identifying Hispanic, I always felt looked down upon but hanging with these new friends carried a new level of respect.

When I wasn't hanging out with Jana and the goat ropers, I still had my one Mexican friend Rosa that I always hung out with. She was eighteen, and I was fifteen when we started to hang out, but I didn't care. I liked hanging out with older friends. One night Rosa and I went out and got drunk. As you can tell by now, that's quite the reoccurring theme in my life.

One night after partying, we went back to my house, and we laid down a pallet of blankets to sleep on the floor. Tammy was already sleeping in the bed, so I thought. Rosa and I were whispering, laughing, and giggling. The next thing I know, Rosa plants one on me. I was pretty much in shock because I hadn't expected it to happen. Tammy jumped out of bed, flung on the light, and said she was telling mom. She went straight to her room and told her what had just happened, and of course, my mom threw a fit. My mom kicked Rosa out of the house and started throwing the Bible at me. Not literally, but she was throwing out scriptures and telling me it was a sin to be gay, and how could I have done that.

I wasn't retaining or even listening to anything she's saying because I'm drunk. Never once did she address the fact that I was fifteen and drunk (welcome to Hispanic culture). The next day, I told her I was sorry about what happened with Rosa, I was drunk, and it would never happen again. She told me I was never allowed to hang out with Rosa, nor were we ever to be friends. I told her I wouldn't, mainly just to get her off my case.

Then, to my surprise, she called my dad. She told me I was going to see my dad because I've got some explaining to do. She took me over there, put me in front of my dad, and said, "Tell your dad what you did."

I looked at him, and I couldn't say anything. It wasn't like I had asked for it. But sitting before him was so humiliating. He asked what I did. I mumbled it out, but he didn't understand me. Finally, I said, "I kissed a girl."

He looked at me, then looked at my mom and said, "*Mija,* (my daughter), don't do that."

HAHAHAHA. I still can't help but laugh when I think of my dad's face saying these words. They were so simple and to the point. My mom was furious. I'm not sure what she expected him to say, but it wasn't that. I wonder how many times, as Christians, we overreact in response to people's sins. Sin is some serious business but let's not forget that we all had sinned before Christ washed it away. Maybe we need to respond somewhere in between my parents, "Whoa, listen, I'm not one to judge, but the path you are choosing is destructive."

Chapter 12

But I Liked It

I kissed a girl, and I liked it. I wanted to see where it might take me. However, there was the delicate task of dealing with my mother. She disapproved of such things. No worries, I had handled this kind of situation before when she interrogated us about visiting Dad and Beatrice. It was time to brush up and revive my double life skills. If mom wanted Priscilla, the heterosexual daughter, then that is who I'd be around her. But I wanted something different for myself.

I continued hanging out with Jana, but as the years went by, I would have her drop me off somewhere I could meet up with Rosa during the evening. When I was 15 years old and drunk, I had my first sexual encounter with Rosa. I knew that it wasn't right. It wasn't just about my mom telling me her Bible said it wasn't right. There was something inside of me that told me it was wrong. Now, I understand what I was feeling that night was conviction; the Holy Spirit nudging me to choose a different path.

But did I listen? Nope. I brushed it off and said, what the heck. I didn't care if it was wrong. I liked it, and I was going to do it anyway. It became more and more frequent. I was drinking and having sex. Then, one night while I was buying alcohol with Rosa, my sister Tammy pulled up. Of course, when she saw us together, she went straight home to tell mom. Why did she always have to be such a Goody-goody?

Mom did what she always did when she wasn't sure what to do with me—send me away or pawn me off. This time she did both! She called my *niña* (godmother) and asked if I could spend the summer with her. My *niña* lived six hours away, so she figured that would surely keep me away from *that* girl. At least for the summer.

The problem with religious people is they focus on the sin and not the person. Most people don't tell you, "Hey, sin can be enjoyable but slow your roll because it has some serious consequences." I mean, maybe some people say this, but nobody was saying it to me, not back then. The only thing they ever told me was how I'd be going to hell for kissing a girl. And the Christian who said it the most was my mom, who was shacking up off and on with her baby daddy, who had molested me. Um, what?

Each of us has our own vices. Sin comes in a whole array of flavors. For this reason, I might not understand why you succumb to the sins you do or did, and you might not understand why I succumbed to the sins that I do or did. But one thing is certain; it does not change the fact that sin is sin no matter what it is or who is doing it.

> "*...each person is tempted when they are dragged away by their own evil desire and enticed. Then, after desire has conceived, it gives birth to sin; and sin, when it is full-grown, gives birth to death.*"
> *James 1:14&15 (NIV)*

"Furthermore, just as they did not think it worthwhile to retain the knowledge of God, so God gave them over to a depraved mind, so that they do what ought not to be done." Romans 1:28 (NIV)

The Holy Spirit was convicting me (attempting to show me a different path to choose) that first night with Rosa. But guess what? I didn't want to choose another direction. I liked my way, and I wanted to wander down it, even if it was wrong, because it was the path I was choosing for myself. And God, being the gentleman that He is, allowed me to do so.

Chapter 13

Double Life

While I was staying with my *niña*, her son David, who was the same age as I, introduced me to one of his friends. I decided to fight these feelings toward girls on my own. Maybe if I were with guys, I would no longer want to be with girls. So, I wound up being with this guy for the whole summer. I came home with hickeys, and my mom was perfectly fine with it because they were from a guy.

But no matter how much I tried, I still could not stand to be around men because of the foundation Luis had laid in my life. I didn't trust them. When they got near me or touched me, I felt tense and uncomfortable. Mom still didn't know about the abuse, nor was I planning to tell her. That is when I got the great idea to have a boyfriend *and* a *secret* girlfriend. It was logical in my mind. If mom thought I had a boyfriend, then she'd stop freaking out about Rosa and me. Life could be pleasant again. So that's what I did.

When I was 17, I got a goat roper boyfriend named Cole who drove a big truck, and mom loved that I had a boyfriend. At the same time, Rosa was my girlfriend. She knew I was seeing Cole, and she knew he was just a show to keep my mom off my back. But she didn't realize I was also having sex with Cole. He was a nice guy; he treated me good, we'd get drunk, and I wouldn't care to say no. The problem for me was every time I had sex with Cole; I felt dirty and disgusting. My mind always associated it with everything Luis had done.

There's nothing easy about living a double life. Rosa was the only one who knew the truth, well, most of it. My friends didn't know I was meeting up with Rosa when they would drop me off at places after hanging out. My mom was none the wiser. There were nights I would come home for curfew and then sneak out with Rosa until one or two in the morning. My high school years were one party after another. I have no idea how we came up with all the money for all the alcohol we drank, but it was always present. Then there were the drugs as well. It was in my junior year of high school I was introduced to acid for the first time. I tried any kind of drug you'd give me. I didn't care. A trip away from reality was one I was always willing to take. Things were going well until one night when I asked mom if I could go to a party, and she told me no.

Now she wanted to parent?

I said ok, went to my room, packed my bag, and jumped out the second-story window. Rosa picked me up around the corner and took me to her friends' house in Ducor. They were a couple of gay men. I stayed with them and went to their wedding while I was there. This experience was my first exposure to gay men and the first gay wedding I attended. I didn't go to school. I didn't call my mom. But for whatever reason, after two weeks, I told Rosa I was ready to go home. I walked into the house, and my mom gave me the biggest hug. "I thought I lost you." That was the only thing she said. No punishment.

On Monday, I found myself in the principal's office. He asked if everything was ok at the house. Of course, I said it was. He didn't need to hear about our drama. I had to do a day of detention for two weeks of being absent. That was it! My only punishment was one day of Saturday school.

I'm no expert on parenting since I never had children, but I'm pretty sure when there aren't any consequences for the choices they make, children tend to do as they please and think it's acceptable. I can only speak from experience on the child's side.

Chapter 14

Goodbye Rosa, Hello Lysol

*I*n my senior year, I became more promiscuous with the opposite sex. I'd get drunk, but I didn't know how to say no, so I was date raped a couple of times. I never considered that abuse, but now that I look back, it was. What's worse is that not only was I being taken advantage of, but I was also abusing myself. I knew drinking would lead to sex which was uncomfortable and awkward. I knew I'd feel dirty and degraded afterward, but I could not get out of this self-destructive cycle. The drink was the only thing I knew I could run to that could make it all go away. Except I didn't realize I was hitting the repeat button.

When I was seventeen, Rosa took me to my first gay bar. Back in the 80's gay bars did not card anybody. My double life began affecting Rosa more and more. She became extremely jealous. I wasn't an ugly girl, so when she caught someone checking me out, she would throw a fit, but instead of reacting to that person, she would take it out on me. I was now experiencing a new kind of abuse… physical.

I didn't want to take her abuse, but I didn't want to get rid of her either. I needed her around because she'd buy me all the things my mom couldn't—mostly booze above all else. I didn't tell a soul. Instead, I started hanging out with Cole and my redneck friends more. I told Rosa I was busy and couldn't hang out with her. When someone saw the bruises from Rosa's abuse, I'd say to them I hit my head or something. I'd always make an excuse.

I had no idea how to stop the beatings. I couldn't tell my mom this woman was hitting me because nobody knew I had been in a relationship with her for the past two years- nobody. Instead of walking away from the abuse, I buried myself in it. I broke up with Cole telling him I didn't want to be with anybody. I stopped hanging out with my friends and went to the gay bars instead.

There were so many lies upon lies. I hadn't told my mother about Luis, and no one had a clue about the date rapes, my relationship with Rosa was a secret, along with the abuse.

It was my senior year before I finally 'came out,' at least to my friends- Linda and Michelle. I told them I was gay, and they said they would support me because they still loved me. But I began to distance myself from my friends. It was also around that time when I finally got the courage to break up with Rosa. But that wouldn't be the last of her in my life. She saw me at a bar after we had broken up. I suppose I should have expected such since we frequented the same bars. She was very apologetic and asked me if she could take me home. On the drive home, we got into an argument. No surprise there. She pulled over and kicked me out of the car. Then she tried to run me over- three times! I ended up getting back in the car, and she took me home.

Then, in January, before I turned 18, I went to a gay bar. Anna Garcia showed up; I hadn't seen her in three years. She had been at one of the hardest prisons for women and had just been released. Anna saw me and said, "Hey punk, what are you doing here?" she looked around and said, "Are you?"

"I don't know…I hang out here," I replied since I was still struggling with the idea.

The evening moved along, and I began talking to a girl my age. She was there with her mom and her mom's partner. Then Rosa showed up. She casually walked up and said she wanted to talk to me. I told her I didn't want to talk to her. She pleaded and begged me until I eventually joined her outside. We talked for a few minutes before she decided to bring up the girl I was talking to and start to get jealous. Just as she was about to hit me, I heard a bottle crack. I turned to find Anna Garcia pointing the broken bottle at Rosa as she said, "Get your f-ing hands off her. That punk right there is my little sister. So, if you want to fight someone, you can fight me right now."

Rosa quickly walked away. Anna was like, "That's what I thought, b...."

That night, I went home with the girl I met, her mom, and her mom's girlfriend. Rosa, out of spite, went to my mother and told her I had been going to gay bars for the past two years. I don't know how Rosa knew where the girl lived, but she told my mom, and the next thing I know, my mom came knocking on their door to drag me home. She laid into me the entire drive home, telling me how awful this was. In my mind, all I could think was, *Really? You're going to tell me how I'm the sinner? Are you going to throw everything I'm doing wrong at me?* Of course, I didn't dare say a word. I may have been rebellious, but I wasn't stupid. When your mom is going off in a rage rant, it's not the time to bring up her own faults. I was the only one of my mom's children she hadn't slapped in the face for talking back. There was no way I was about to lose that prize-ha!

She went to church. I have no idea what the church people told her because she came back saying, "You're sick, you're sinning, and you're going to hell. You're not natural."

Gee, great, that's the God I want to serve.

She decided it was best to take me to a mental hospital. She wanted me to sit with a psychiatrist. He asked me a bunch of questions, then brought me back to my mother and told her, "There's nothing wrong with your child. It's you who has the problem."

I found his response comical. She, of course, did not.

So, on to the police department, we went. My mom walked up to the counter and told them she didn't want me explaining that she has six other kids at home and doesn't want me to infect them. Back in the 80's when AIDS had just become very publicized, and there was a lot of fear surrounding the unknowns of this disease. I'm sure those officers enjoyed being pulled into our family drama. They told her they couldn't take me because there were no charges against me.

Do we go home? No. From there, she takes me to child protective services and asks if they can put me in a foster home. All the while, I am right there next to her as she is trying to pawn me away. With each stop, and every word, I am getting more and more numb, but I refuse to shed a single tear. I don't want to give her the privilege of seeing how much she is hurting me.

They told her they could put me in a foster home, but it wouldn't make much sense because I would be eighteen in two months. She took me back to the house and told all my siblings they could not speak to me or be around me. Then she proceeded to follow me around the house with a can of Lysol, spraying everything I touched and everywhere I went.

My youngest sister Anya, who was three years old, would sit across the room and stare at me. The hardest part was when she would sit by my bedroom door and cry because she could no longer love on me.

It broke my heart. I called the girl I'd met at the bar and asked if I could stay with them. Then, I checked myself out of high school. When I got back to the house, mom had a heart change and told me I could continue living at the house. So, I went back to the school and checked myself back in. They, of course, asked if everything was ok at home. "Oh, it's just peachy."

I'm not sure why I believed it would work. Maybe I had hoped it would. But after a week of continued separation and

Lysol trails, I returned to the school to check myself out. I got checked in at the new high school and moved in with the girl from the bar, her mom, and her mom's girlfriend. I had to attend a new high school four months before graduation, was miserable. It wasn't all bad, though, because my girlfriend's mom let us do whatever we wanted. Living here was my first experience at shacking up, and because it was in a gay environment, my confusion only thickened.

My mom had no idea she was throwing me right into the devil's arms. She wanted me to know the gay lifestyle was wrong, yet they were the only ones openly showing me love and acceptance. On the day of my eighteenth birthday, my mom came knocking on their door. She told me she would learn to live with my same-sex attraction. She loved me and wanted me to move back home. It all sounded good. Who doesn't want to be accepted and loved by their parents?

I checked myself back into my high school. I bet those people in the office were getting whiplash from seeing me so much that year. I continued to stay with my girlfriend on the weekends and ride the Greyhound back to my house for the school week. Despite all the craziness, I finally made it to graduation. Can you believe it? Me either! I went to the biggest grad party and lived it up before going home after a heavy night of partying. The next morning I'm still trying to recoup, and mom hit's me with this wonderful statement, "Go straight or get out."

I went to the kitchen, grabbed some paper bags, went straight to my room, filled the bags with my clothes, and moved out, never to return. I stayed with my girlfriend for a little while but having to deal with her mom was like dealing with my mom, and I couldn't take two mothers nagging me about different things. So, I broke things off with her.

After that, I moved in with an old friend from school. We began dating, and I helped her raise her son. We started partying more and more. One night, while we were drinking, we started playing quarters with a gallon of vodka. I had two people ganging up on me, so by the time it was all over, I had drunk half of that gallon by myself. I sat in the corner of the room, throwing up. The next morning, I was still there, unable to throw up anything else. Just dry heaves over and over. They figured I had a hangover, but I didn't get out of the corner for four days. None of us knew what alcohol poisoning was. I should have been dead. I know I have been close to death six times in my life, and this was one of them. By the grace of God, He still protected me even in my hedonistic lifestyle.

So often, we are tempted by things because they seem so good. Try some alcohol; it will make you feel good. Try some sex, and it will make you feel good. Well, duh, it will! People don't continue to go back to it because it makes them feel like crap. But for some reason, we forget the awful pain and regret these things cause. I almost died but hey, no big deal, let's have another drink tomorrow.

Chapter 15

Anya And El Coco

I mentioned how hard it was to leave my baby sister, Anya, when my mom kicked me out of the house at eighteen, but I need to back up for a moment. When I was 15, my mom got pregnant again by Luis. I hated her when I found out she was pregnant by him. See, when she was pregnant with Louie, I didn't know how babies came about or much about sex. But this time, I did, and it disgusted me to think of her having sex with such an awful, disgusting man. I said her baby was the devil's spawn. And I called her that until she was born. That was the moment she stole my heart. I loved her so much. In my eyes, there was no way she could possibly be Luis's child. She was so precious, innocent, and beautiful. I'd rock her to sleep; she was my little baby. I loved everything about her. By the time she was old enough to walk, she would follow me all around the house. She was like my little kid.

I never EVER wanted Luis to molest her, so from the moment she started talking, I would whisper in her ear, "Your daddy is the *El Coco* (monster)." I had her so convinced that every time Luis would stop by the house and get near her, she would scream at the top of her lungs. He'd ask my mom what was wrong with her, and my mom would say she didn't know. Then, after he left, she'd climb on my lap, and I would say, "Good job, you screamed so loud the *El Coco* couldn't get you."

You might see it as an awful mind game, but I know I saved my sister from being molested because Luis went on to have other daughters, and they were all molested. What do they say? Drastic times call for drastic measures. I will never regret the extreme actions I took to protect my little sister.

Chapter 16

Palm Springs and Claire

Anya was a gorgeous little kid; when she was five, my mom entered her in a pageant in Palm Springs. She asked me if I wanted to join them on the trip. My Aunt Lupe was entering her daughter in the pageant as well, so it would be the five of us on this road trip. I didn't really want to go, but somehow mom convinced me. When I got there, I was bored to death. I didn't want to hang out with them doing all their girlie pageant stuff. So, I hopped a cab to a gay piano bar. Because it was 2 PM when I arrived, there weren't many people at the bar: just me and one other person. Then Claire showed up.

Little did I realize this thirty-two-year-old woman was about to change my life. She walked into the bar with her classy clothes and her high heels clicking across the floor, followed by two men. The two men accompanying her were her boyfriend's brothers. They brought me into their conversation like we were old friends. She looked at me and asked me why I was gay. She didn't have an issue with me being gay, but she didn't think I was. In her words, "You're way too pretty to be gay."

We talked and continued drinking there until 5 or 6 that night. I told them I was going to head out, and Claire offered me a ride back to the hotel. She said to me on the ride that she and Jeff, her boyfriend, were broken up at the moment because he was acting like a jerk. We hung out at the hotel bar for a while before I was invited back to her house for dinner. She drove out of Palm Springs into the desert, and I thought, *Oh, god, this woman is going to kill me.* But she didn't. We wound up in a small town called White Water. We had dinner, we had an affair, and then we went to sleep.

Then, after midnight on July 8, 1986, at 2:20 AM, a 6.0 earthquake hit White Water, California. We jumped out of bed. The house was rumbling, and everything was falling apart around us. It was a disaster. The fireplace was in the middle of the living room, and so many things were broken around. We were unable to get out of the house due to the door jams that had buckled. Since it was pitched dark outside when we finally made it out of the house, I fell over a tree torn out of the ground. Around six in the morning, Jeff showed up to pick up Claire. She introduced us, and he said he'd take me to the hotel. When we got to the hotel, everyone was standing outside in the parking lot wrapped in blankets. Mom was furious; she jumped all over me. Despite all the commotion, we were back in Porterville by that afternoon.

I'm pretty sure I never told Claire my last name. That's just not something you do with a one-night stand. But somehow, despite the lack of Google and social media, she sent me a huge bouquet of two dozen roses two weeks later. The card attached said:

I hope you're ok and I hope you made it home. Love, C

I wasn't quite sure how in the world this woman found me, but the bouquet was beautiful. My mom was ticked when those roses showed up at her house because she knew they were from a lesbian encounter. It was the first time my lifestyle was in her face, but it was also the first time I had received flowers. The card included her phone number so I could call her, which I did.

A few months later, she sent me an airline ticket to fly back to Palm Springs. That was my first plane ride. Claire and Jeff had reconciled, and they were now living together. Jeff picked me up at the airport then we met up with Claire for dinner. This was the first time I was exposed to people with any kind of money. There was no counting to see if you had enough before choosing what you wanted from the menu. It was a different kind of scene from what I was used to, and I found myself very insecure but also drawn to the stuff.

On this trip, I soon learned that Claire did not have an ounce of lesbian in her. Our one-night stand was nothing more than a fling. She was still convinced I needed a good experience with a man, so that is what she tried to create with her and Jeff. I didn't know it at the time, but this would be my first experience with swingers. Being with Jeff wasn't as bad as my previous experiences with men because Claire was there. My week stay involved a lot of cocaine, drinking, and sexual escapades with both of them.

I flew home, and she'd call bi-weekly to check up on me. All I ever did was party with the drag queens who lived across the street from my dad. They were a fascinating bunch. One day she asked, "What are you doing with your life? Are you just going to hang out with those drag queens and get drunk for the rest of your life?"

I replied, "What else is there to do in this town?"

She said, "Pack your bags. Jeff and I will be there in four hours to pick you up."

I said, "It's 9:30 at night."

She said, "Yes, we'll be there in four hours."

I hung up the phone and said, "Hey, dad, I'm moving out." The thought of packing my things and moving didn't even phase me. By this time in my life, I had moved so many times I had lost count.

Around one in the morning, Claire and Jeff knocked on the door to pick me up. We got back to their house at six in the morning. Claire showed me which room would be mine, and I crashed. The next morning, she said, "What happened in the past is in the past. There will be no more sexual encounters in this house. You're going to find a job and make something of yourself. Until then, you're going to help me at the house and with Ian." Ian was her six-year-old son. She had joint custody with her ex-husband.

Jeff and his brothers owned a construction company; I went to work for them building roads, shoveling asphalt, learning how to operate backhoes and loaders. It wasn't anything permanent. I'd only go to work with them every once in a while to make some chump change. There was an ad in the paper for UPS, hiring for various positions. Claire said, "I want you to apply for UPS. That's a good place to work, they have good benefits, and you'll make good money."

I applied, had an interview, and every day after, Claire would come home and ask if I called human resources. "I want you to call every week to remind them who you are. They have to remember who you are and see you want this job."

Claire was giving me discipline and motherly direction. I had never had this kind of encouragement and support in my life. No one ever told me I would make something of myself while I was in their house, no one except Claire. I had never seen ambitious people, people who ran their own business until I met Claire and Jeff.

I got hired on at UPS. I was a part-time clerk, and she was delighted with that. She said, "It doesn't matter where you start. It matters where you end."

I lived with her and Jeff for a year, and then she said I needed to be on my own. They had a couple of acres on Palm Springs' outskirts, where they kept all the construction business equipment. There was a single wide mobile home on the property that they moved me into, and this was the first time I lived independently.

My mom had never been an instructive mother. Her idea of school was to go if you want or skip if you wanted. Just don't come home crying to her if you got caught ditching. She never spoke about college. She told me a whole bunch of religious things but never taught me any life skills to better myself. Maybe she didn't know what to teach me since she never graduated high school.

Claire had such a significant impact on my life. She took me, a girl wasting her life away partying, and molded me into a successful businesswoman who now had a vision of an obtainable future on the horizon.

Chapter 17

The Abortion

Jeff and Claire invited me to join them at a classic car auction in Newport Beach. They were going to auction Jeff's dad's 1963 red Thunderbird. We were staying in a hoity-toity hotel. It was there in Newport that the three of us had another escapade.

She convinced Jeff and me to have an affair without her first before the three of us did anything. She wanted me to have a heterosexual encounter so he could show me the difference between abuse and being taken care of. The problem with carefree sex is that it is just that- carefree. You do it when you want to with who you want to, and you think very little of any consequences your actions might bring.

Consequently, this led to a private affair between Jeff and me. It went on for months without Claire knowing about it. Then I got pregnant. When she found out I was pregnant, she asked if Jeff was the father. I told her he wasn't, even though he and I knew that was a lie. I asked Jeff what I was going to do. He came to the construction yard and left me $300 for an abortion.

In February 1987, a friend accompanied me to the abortion clinic. I was so nervous, but there were several reasons I had determined I could not keep the baby. The first and most important reason in my mind was that I didn't want the baby to come out looking like Jeff. Claire had taken me in and taught me how to live on my own. I couldn't do that to her. My following reason was that I had sworn to myself, I would never have a kid and put it on welfare. The last reason was that I wanted my mom's genes to stop here.

By this time, I was like two months and twenty-nine days pregnant. I had terrible morning sickness and couldn't even brush my teeth without gagging. I was terrified and had waited as long as I absolutely could, which is why I got cold feet. I was sitting there alone in the room, in a gown, about to have an abortion, scared to death. While the nurse had stepped out, I changed back into my clothes and walked down the hallway. Before I could escape, the nurse stopped me. She was an awful woman with no bedside manners. She asked me what I was doing. When I told her I couldn't do it, she told me to get back in that room. If I put this off, I would no longer be able to have an abortion and be stuck with having the baby, and I would regret it. Tomorrow would be too late. Once again, I felt as if my voice had been taken away from me. I felt super powerless. So, I went back into the room, changed back into the gown, and laid there on that table, with tears rolling down my face as they sucked my baby out of me. When it was all over, that horrible, awful nurse had the nerve to tell me, "Oh, by the way, it was a girl." She was a wretch of a woman.

I went home and got drunk. Drinking was the only way I knew how to deal with pain. I drank and drank and drank until I was numb, until I no longer felt…anything. Jeff and I never had an affair again. It ended just like that.

Let's review. Trying to stop sin with sin doesn't work. Trying to resolve abuse with adultery also not a good choice. Everything Claire had hoped to achieve by having me sleep with Jeff backfired. I was now even more confused about how I should feel about men. Jeff had used me just like Luis had used me, only this time I had consented to the relationship.

And just like that, from one chapter to the next, we can go from admiring the lessons we're taught to questioning what the heck we just endured. Claire and Jeff continued to be a significant part of my life for quite a few years until we eventually grew apart.

Chapter 18

I'm Gay

*A*fter the abortion, I started becoming very promiscuous with men and women. I had just turned twenty-one, so I was at all the bars—straight bars, gay bars—it made no difference to me. I was legal, and life was one big party in Palm Springs. All the while, I was wrestling with my sexuality. Sex with women didn't seem quite right, but it wasn't as a chore as sex with men. With men, I couldn't even think about having sex unless I was drunk. And then, the only reason I would continue is that I was drunk and wouldn't say no. I found myself caught in a vicious cycle of self-abuse.

Claire had told me numerous times that she didn't think I was gay. She was convinced I just needed to find the right man. She played a significant role in my life; I trusted her and had such a deep respect for her. Unfortunately, her pushing Jeff at me had only made matters worse. Now I was living with lies, cover-up, and an unborn baby on my hands.

Despite all my escapades, I maintained my job at UPS. I suppose all that proves is you can be all kind of messed up inside and come across to everyone else as an average functioning human. Around my 22nd birthday, I met two people, a crossroads of sorts. One was Jill, a bartender at the comedy club I attended on my birthday that year. The other was Mike Deluca, an ex-Chippendale dancer; he was a hunk of a man! I was seeing both of them for a while. Until we all ran into each other at the store one day- that was a little awkward. "Oh yeah, this is…" Nobody wants to have that kind of conversation.

I eventually broke things off with Mike because I couldn't get comfortable with him. No matter how dreamy he was, no matter how much I wanted to make it work, there was still something that constantly threw up a barricade between me and any man I tried to get close to. After breaking things off with Mike, I continued dating Jill and pledged to myself that was the end of men.

It was at this time; I made the decision I was gay. I was going to accept who I was and be proud of who I was. My mom called me numerous times, and she always asked me questions like when I was going to go straight and get married. I finally got the courage to set a healthy boundary for myself. "Mom, this is who I am. If you can't accept that, if you can't call me without asking these questions, then don't bother to call me."

She didn't call me for six months. When she finally did call me, I told her I could only talk with her if she stopped nagging me. Remember, this is the same kind of relationship she had with her mother. She lived a life that she wanted, and her mom constantly nagged her about her choices. Now she was doing the same thing with her daughter.

Toxicity only produces toxicity. If we want to be free from the bondage of this world—even if it seems something simple and insignificant as a nagging mother/daughter relationship—we have to do things God's way.

Chapter 19

Jack (Daniels) and Jill

Unbeknownst to me, Jill was an alcoholic and had a cocaine addiction. Although I'd do drugs if they were offered, I would never buy any. I thought they were a waste of money. My hard-earned cash should be invested in smarter things—like alcohol.

Because she was a bartender, a benefit of dating her was all drinks on the house. Man, I saved so much money not having to buy alcohol, and I loved having extra money to spend! The downfall was that our relationship was chaotic, to say the least. Cocaine was always lying around the house, and we were always partying. We were at parties, and people were always at our home drinking. There was never a moment of silence. The relationship was so toxic, but I "cared" for her. She would leave for two weeks at a time, and I wouldn't know where she went or when she'd be back. I'd be worried sick about her. I began to realize just how bad her addiction was and began to worry about her more and more.

Then one day, after she'd been gone for two weeks, she came back home and fell on the floor. I called 911. They told me she was dying. They said she was malnourished and dehydrated.

If she didn't get help, she would kill herself from the choices she was making. I didn't know anything about rehab or counseling or any kind of substance abuse programs one could use to detox. So, I rented a room at a hotel in the desert and kept her there. Welcome to Priscilla's Pampering for Pushers. You pop it; we stop it!

Oh my gosh, I had no idea what I was doing. Here I was, an alcoholic in denial trying to help a drug addict detox. I'd lock the door and go to work, leaving her at the hotel. She couldn't call anybody, so I wasn't worried about her leaving, and I was pretty sure she didn't want to leave.

During this time, I found out her home life was just as messed up as mine. Maybe even a little more messed up in my eyes. Her dad had cheated on her mom. But the worst part of the affair was that he would take her and her brother to meet up with his mistress. He'd lock them in the trunk while they did whatever they did. Then when her brother got older, he and his friends raped her. She was from the East Coast and had moved to California to escape her family.

I kept her in that hotel room for about a month before she started to look and sound good. Then we went back to Palm Springs. She found another bartending job, and a few months later, the process started all over again. I was so over it by this time that I cheated on her and eventually broke up with her.

Let this be a lesson that hurting people cannot help people. I had no business trying to help Jill work through her issues. I hadn't even acknowledged and addressed my own.

Chapter 20

"Lesbeans"

D o you know what the greatest lesbian joke is? What do lesbians bring on their second date? A UHAUL! Oh—and it's so true!

So, rather than fill this book with all my crazy escapades, I'll sum up the majority of it in this chapter. You already know that I was fifteen when I had my first girl/girl encounter, and I was forty-five when I got saved. For those thirty years in-between, I had a new girlfriend about every two years. I traded them out like I traded my vehicles. And sometimes, I gave them a car or Seadoos just to get rid of them. I guess that's what happens when you're the one making more money and owning the homes.

It was never a simple matter of leaving them either. Most of the time, I would end the relationship by cheating or just being mean. They would end up being too needy in my mind, and I would decide that meant it was ok to sleep with someone else. The main reason I felt this way was because anything that felt too normal was wrong.

I also began hanging out with other lesbians as well. Birds of a feather flock together, right? You want to be around people who are going to accept you the way you are. I had my little lesbian delivery driver posse that I began hanging out with every weekend. By this time, I was a UPS delivery driver, and so were all my friends; however, there were a couple of FedEx drivers and a postal worker. Later, when I went into management with UPS and had moved to Riverside, CA, I had a new bunch of friends, and we would have weekend parties. One particular time we came out of the house, and the kids across the street put a sign on the mailbox, "Lesbeans." We laughed so hard because of the way they spelled it. But that was my first experience of being targeted for my lifestyle outside of my family.

Homosexuality throws around what they call big love. Everybody loves anybody, but it isn't about love at all. It's about sex, lust and never being alone. I can promise you you're not born that way. I had accepted and convinced myself I was, in fact, born that way. I would even tell my mother this. How could God default me for being born gay? I now know I was molested gay.

Chapter 21

The Sperm Donor

I mentioned in an earlier chapter the issues between my dad and me. After he'd cheated on Bea, I didn't want anything to do with him for a time. When I got older, I had moved in with him for a little while before Claire and Jeff took me in. Little did I know our issues weren't over.

In 1997, my mother called me out of the blue and asked if I wanted to attend her cousin's daughter's wedding in Arizona. I barely knew her side of the family out there, but a road trip didn't sound that bad. I had just spent the last year undergoing extensive surgery on both my feet, which ended up leaving me 65% disabled. A change of scenery would be just what I needed.

She'd asked my sister Tammy to come along. Tammy was now a mother of three and living in Sacramento, so of course, spending time with my sister sweetened the deal even more. Then, for whatever reason, she called my dad and asked if he wanted to go as well.

Here we are, just the four of us on our way to Arizona. Our first "family" road trip. My dad was also an alcoholic, so we asked my mom to pull over for us to buy some beer. Here we are, drinking beer in the backseat on this road trip. We got to

Phoenix, and my dad wanted to see his brother. So, the four of us headed over to Uncle Mike's house.

My dad said, "Hey, you remember Linky and Tammy?"

"What Slinky Linky? Oh, you're all grown up." My uncle replied. Then we went into the normal 'haven't seen you in forever' kind of family conversations. He asked Tammy if she was married, and she told him she was, and now she had three kids—blah, blah, blah, life is good. Then he turns to me, "What about you, Linky, you married?"

I said, "No, I'm gay."

Remember back to the "Don't do that, *Mija*." conversation my dad had after the first time I kissed a girl? Well, that was the only time he ever said anything about my lifestyle. Other than that time, he would not acknowledge it in any way, shape, or form.

By this time, both my dad and I are buzzed. I was loud and proud; I didn't care who knew I was gay. But my dad's face turned to beat red. I'm not sure if he was angry or embarrassed or both that I had so openly admitted I was gay, but he was furious. My mom's eyes widened as if she could not believe what I had just done. But my uncle's only reply was, "Oh…that's nice."

We went on to the wedding, nothing was said about the matter. But this was a Hispanic wedding, so of course, it's loud and rowdy and stocked with plenty of beer. Mom was off visiting with the family she rarely saw, and Tammy was out on the dancefloor. That left dad and me sitting at the table drinking. I have no idea what the conversation was about, but I remember him slapping me across the face and calling me a lesbian bitch.

You might be quick to blame the alcohol, but my dad was always a happy guy to be around, even when he was drunk. I could call him up right now and be laughing within minutes because he's such a fun guy, so I am unsure where that came from that day. I looked at him and said, "From this day forward, you are no longer my dad. You are my sperm donor." Then I marched out onto the dance floor and told Tammy, "Dad just slapped me across the face and called me a lesbian bitch."

While I may have been mom's favorite, Tammy was always dad's favorite. Remember the jewelry he got her for her eighteenth birthday? Tammy's not drinking; she didn't like that out-of-control feeling which I never understood. But she stormed across that dance floor like a crazed drunk as she walked straight up to my dad and slapped him across the face. She said, "Don't you ever put your hand on my sister again."

If it had been any other wedding reception, there probably would have been a moment of silence when everyone started wondering what had just happened. But since this was a loud Hispanic wedding, the only people who noticed were the few sitting near us. We went up to mom, told her we had to leave and left dad at the wedding. I still have no idea how he got himself back to California.

When I got home, I was intent on changing my name. When I told him he was no longer my dad, I had meant it. I didn't want anything to do with him. I told my girlfriend at the time that I wanted to change my last name. I didn't care what it was, but it couldn't be Murillo. She suggested using hers. After asking her parents, that's precisely what I did. I went through the process of legally changing my last name to Priscilla Peckham. After it was changed, I made sure my dad got word I was no longer Priscilla Murillo.

Changing my last name was certainly not a "vengeance is mine sayth the Lord moment." (Romans 12:19) It was Priscilla's vengeance, and you're going to pay kind of moment. You might know the saying, hurting people *hurt* people. Well, it is true. There was not a single drop of remorse or forgiveness in my heart at that moment. In fact, I didn't speak to my dad for four years after that incident.

I broke up with that girlfriend in 2000 and kept the last name for another two years before changing it to my real name. I say we broke up, but it was all sabotaged by me as usual. Things were just way too good to be okay. She came from a good family. Her parents had a long-lasting relationship, and her grandparents had been married for sixty years—sixty years! She had this well-balanced kind of life. It was all too...normal. So, I cheated on her.

That was my signature move. If anything was going well in a relationship, I had to demolish it. I was self-destructive because I was under the illusion this led to self-preservation. If I was the one to break it off, there was no room for me to get hurt. Like 'em and leave 'em one right after the other because there certainly wasn't any kind of love. I had no idea what love was. How could I offer up something I knew nothing about?

Chapter 22

Jumping Off the AA Wagon

was living a life filled with so much denial. I had convinced myself I was born gay, and I most certainly was not an alcoholic. Alcoholics were people who drank every day; I didn't drink every day. So, when one of my friends told me I should join her at an AA meeting, that was my response.

She said, "It's not about drinking every day, Priscilla. It's about what you do when you're drinking. Do you ever wake up ashamed?"

"Well, of course, we all do."

"Can you stop when you want to stop?"

Now she had me because I didn't know the meaning of 'just one more.' She planted these seeds in my head. Everything she was saying made me think about and realize how tired I was of all this partying and drinking. All this searching for something that I still had yet to find nothing could fill the hole. I had been doing this since I was a teenager, and now, I was in my 30's. She invited me again, and I decided to attend. Until I realized they were meeting in a church building. I said, "Hell no, I'm not going in there!"

I didn't realize AA had two types of meetings. Anyone could attend a public meeting, and you didn't have to acknowledge you were an alcoholic. In a private meeting, like the one I had been invited to, participants were required to admit they were alcoholics. My hands were sweating so bad as I followed her into this church. She hadn't prepared me for anything, so the whole time we are walking in to take our seats, I'm thinking, "Ok, maybe if I go, I can learn to control my drinking. Yes, I will go to learn to control it but not stop drinking because that would be too boring."

I have zero intentions of admitting I am an alcoholic and give up my drinking completely. My friend introduced me to all her little AA buddies. They were all straight women from Huntington Beach, and they didn't act like any of my friends. I sat down, and they start going around the room, "My name is_____, and I'm an alcoholic."

They got to me, and I said, "My name's Priscilla."

They all stared at me for a moment, probably wondering who is this woman in denial was. I had just crashed their private meeting. Then they stood up in a circle, held hands, and began to pray, "God grant me the serenity to…"

I was pissed, absolutely fuming. If I wanted to go to church, I would have gone to church. I didn't come here for that. I came to help control my drinking. Despite my frustration, I stayed and listened to what they had to say. They ended the meeting holding hands once more, then after saying the Lord's Prayer, they stated, "Keep coming back; it works if you work it."

I was like, "What kind of BS is this? I've been pulled into a cult." And that was that; I didn't go back. But six months later, I once again felt worn out with the life I was living. So, I called my friend, "Can AA help me control my drinking?"

I went back and started listening to everything they were saying. I received a Newcomer's Chip, and they said, "You're not going to drink today."

Ok, can I drink tomorrow?

I started going to meetings three times a week and soon began to think I could do this non-drinking thing. It wasn't so bad. I was three months sober when I decided to get a sponsor. They always told us our sponsor should be someone who you want what they have. I chose Debbie. She had been sober for twelve years! I had always admired her when she would speak at the meetings. She certainly had something I wanted. When I asked if she would be my sponsor, she said, "Ok, but you have to promise me a few things."

"What's that?"

"You have to be willing to take instructions."

I said, "Ok, I'll take instructions."

She said, "Remember everything I tell you is instructions, not commands. You can choose to do it or don't."

I feel kind of bad thinking back to Debbie. She had no idea what she was getting herself into when she became my sponsor. She probably felt like she was dealing with a five-year-old most of the time. I was emotionally jacked up, yet here I was, trying to sober up *without Jesus*. I'm sure it was like trying to take Tarzan and turn him into a man.

Debbie had me call her every day and tell her how I was doing. She had structure and rules. She was very wise and used that wisdom to work with me. They continued to allow me to attend the private meeting even though I couldn't say I was an alcoholic. Debbie was high on the totem pole and asked them to give me some time. The first time I acknowledged in a meeting that I was an alcoholic was probably two months in, and those were the hardest words to come out of my mouth.

"Hi, my name is Priscilla, and I am an alcoholic."

After I had been going for sixth months, I told my mom I was going to AA and had a sponsor named Debbie. She rebuked me and asked why I thought I was an alcoholic. AA was a cult.

I said, "Mom, I am an alcoholic, and I'm trying to get help."

Debbie was my sponsor for three years, and my mom did not like the fact that I had a woman in my life giving me instructions. Claire had given me business and life skills, whereas Debbie showed me what it was like to get a backbone. She was teaching me I didn't have to numb myself every single time something went wrong or I 'just had a day.' She was a great sponsor, and she showed me so much, love.

I started hanging out with all those women even though they weren't like me. I stopped going to the bars and started going to the movies with them. I even joined in on their luncheons! There was happiness and peace I found with these ladies. I was nervous and afraid at first, but I found comfort with them. All these ladies just loved me. I would walk in, and they would give me the tightest hugs. Genuine affection with no sexual ties whatsoever. Just sisterhood. That's what I found in them.

When Sheila Patrick moved away in the eighth grade, I had lost touch with her. But when I was thirty-three, we found ourselves connected once again. Then one evening, she knocked on the door. There before me stood my old friend, so many years had passed since we saw each other. We laughed and caught up on life. Then, right there on the spot, she said, "Priscilla, would you be my maid of honor?"

It was such a special moment for me. My sister Tammy and I had always talked about being in each other's weddings, but when she got married, my mom would not allow me to be in the wedding since I had decided I was gay. I snuck into the church and sat in the back row for my sister's wedding.

Here Sheila was asking me to be her maid of honor. What an honor it was!

By this time, I had already completed my 12 steps, and I'm sponsoring other women in the program. It wasn't an easy task. It had taken me six months to get through step three of the program because that step involved God, and you know how I felt about God. I told Debbie I was going to Chico for a wedding and flew out there nine days before my 3rd sobriety birthday.

Although this was Sheila's second wedding, it was a beautiful wedding; I still have all the pictures. The wedding took place seven days before my 3rd sobriety birthday. I'm at the reception, and suddenly I get the urge to drink something. I call my sponsor, Debbie, no answer. I call other ladies in my group, no response. I even called my girlfriend at the time, who had never seen me touch alcohol. Nobody answered their phones!

That's when I decided I wanted to do what I wanted to do. So, I drank, and I got drunk.

Debbie had always told me, "Priscilla, if you go out, the door doesn't always swing back." I never quite understood what that meant until after that night of drinking. I called my girl-friend and told her I had got drunk. Then I made the call I was dreading—the call to Debbie.

She said, "I'm not going to tell you that I'm not disap-pointed because I'm very disappointed. But I love you, and you will start over. Tonight, when you go to the meeting, you will pick up a Newcomer's chip."

Picking up that Newcomer's chip was such a humiliating experience. Why, after three years, had I decided to drink? I stayed sober, again, up until seven days before my 1st-year sobriety mark. After that, I detached from the entire group.

I didn't understand that you will eventually fail when you try to do things through your own willpower. Jesus said in *John 15:5*, *"Apart from me you can do nothing."* That's true on so many levels.

Chapter 23

The Jesus Freak

I met Donna Castaneda while I was working at American Electronics Resources. She was a white lady married to a Mexican man. And guess what? She was a Christian. I could spot a Christian at a thousand paces, and this is one of the first things I picked up about her because she wasn't *just* a Christian. She was a Jesus freak! Because of conversations that would pop up here and there, I knew she was a holy roller, Pentecostal, speaking in tongues, kind of Christian. Whenever I learned someone was a Christian, my initial thought was to assume they were a Bible reading, pew sitting kind of person. Donna wasn't that way. She wasn't this goodie-two-shoes Christian that condemned my lifestyle. She treated me normal and with respect. She didn't flaunt her religion or push it on me. Because of this, we developed a friendship. I'd say, "Hey, Freak," obviously short for Jesus freak. But Donna never budged on her beliefs. She accepted the nickname with grace and never preached to me…ever.

We'd been working together for two years when one day she walked into my office and said, "Priscilla, I have to tell you something."

I looked up and said, "Ok."

She got really nervous, said, "Oh no, I can't." Then walked out of the office. She repeated this a few times before she took a deep breath and said, "I have to. God wants me to tell you something."

My defense mechanism instantly went up. I set my legs on my desk, crossed them, leaned back in the chair, and crossed my arms in front of my chest. "Oh really? What does your God want you to tell me?"

I knew what she was about to say; I'd heard it once before from all the other Christians. But to my surprise, she didn't say the typical thing.

Instead, she said, "God wants me to tell you that you are not going to heaven because of your lesbianism; you're going to hell because of your hard heart."

I replied, "Oh, is that so."

I overlooked her comment, partially because I didn't understand her statement. She was the first Christian not to condemn my lifestyle. That was always, always, the go-to condemnation from Christians. "You're going to hell because you're a lesbian." What did she mean I was going to hell because I had a hard heart?

I used to tell my mother, "I'd rather go to hell than be in heaven with you Christians." That was the distaste I had for them. They were always talking about God's love then casting all the gays into hell with the next breath. It was so two-faced in my eyes. How can you say your God loves people but only if they are straight? What kind of God is this? By this time in my life, the Jesus I knew from my youth was so far in the distant past... I was now anti-God, anti-religion, anti-Bible, and anti-Christ.

It wasn't until years later, when I became a Christian, that I began to realize God really did love people, even lesbians. He simply had no tolerance for sin. Not from homosexuals, not from straight people, not from anybody. But I'll talk about this more in a later chapter.

Chapter 24

You Cannot Run from You

You know there's that saying, "What goes around comes around."

Well, when you're sleeping around and having affairs to get out of your relationships, it's probably only a matter of time before that comes back to bite you. And that is precisely what it did. I was head over heels for my new girlfriend, Kori. Things were good when they were good, but when things were not going well, she had a habit of leaving and going back to her ex-girlfriend. What kind of person does this sort of thing?

In all my relationships, I had always been the dumper; no one had ever dumped me. But this one dumped me! What was happening? Every other ex, I would simply drink away and soon forget about them, but Kori was different. She'd come and go, be gone then back. Her leaving me for her ex-girlfriend really did me in.

One night, she was on one of her missing in action moments. I was walking my dogs down the street, and I was tired, mentally, and emotionally exhausted. This lifestyle had no meaning, no stability. Here I was thirty-nine years old, and it was wearing on me. There were no true friends, and I was beginning to feel hollow inside.

That night I looked up at the stars and said, "God, if you are real, I'm tired of this lifestyle. Take this woman out of my life." Nothing spectacular happened at that moment, but for me to speak out to 'maybe God', I was at a low for sure.

On New Year's Eve 2004, Kori moved out. Around July, my sister Tammy called me and told me she had found out her husband, Cory, had been having an ongoing affair. Man, we both had "Cory/Kori" issues because I still hadn't quite gotten over mine either. She was still in and out, here and there, toying with my heart.

I decided my sister needed me. She was falling apart; I was falling apart. Maybe it would feel better if we fell apart together. I flew to Texas and arrived the day after Hurricane Katrina had hit them. When I saw the costs of homes in Texas, I was impressed. I had just sold my house in California, so I put an offer on a place and flew back to pack my things.

Yes, Tammy was falling apart, and I felt needed in her life, but my real motive for leaving California was to get away from it all. Everything. The partying, the alcohol, the women, the emptiness. I wanted a change. After watching my mom for so many years, I should have realized that leaving a place wouldn't fix the problem if the issue was in your own heart. I couldn't get to Texas and expect everything to be fixed because where you go, there you are.

Three days after I arrived in Texas, I talked my sister into going with me to a Gretchen Wilson concert in The Woodlands. I'm drinking at the concert, so of course, I have to pee, and while we're standing in line for the bathroom, we meet a group of lesbians. Since I was new in town, these ladies invited me to join them at a club called The Ranch House after the concert. Then just like that, I jumped right back into everything I had run away from.

I ended up meeting this woman named Stephanie. Here's my advice, never EVER meet somebody when you are drunk and then expect a healthy relationship. Because they will be a completely different person when you're sober, and you will probably not like them. Stephanie was great, but I soon realized she was an alcoholic. I had attended AA meetings, so the thought of being an alcoholic lingered on my mind because I could never get control over my drinking. But this woman, on the other hand—she was out of control even for me.

Even though I was with Stephanie, alcoholism was right in my face; I couldn't face the truth. I couldn't accept my failure. I had failed at so many things over the years. The last thing I wanted to do was linger on my AA failure. I had failed my parents by coming out as a lesbian. I had failed my relationships, and nothing seemed to last, even the really good ones. I had gone three years, THREE YEARS, without drinking only to fall off that wagon. And there had been no getting back on it. I tried and tried but could never seem to get past the 90-day sober mark. I'd remember my failure and think, "What's the point of trying?"

The only long-lasting job I had was with UPS. That had lasted ten years, and I'd been robbed by disability. I had tried to fill the emptiness in my life with anything and everything imaginable except Jesus. Keep that nasty religious stuff away from me!

With every failure, I would ask myself, "Why am I here?" Not in a suicidal way but from an empty purposeless place. I was living a life of dead existence and had no idea. I'm not the only one. So many people try to fill that void with bars, sex, relationships, material things and find themselves even more empty when none of it works.

Chapter 25

You're Not Gay

*H*ere I am once again sitting in my singleness. I have a boat; I have a brand-new house. In 2006, I put an inground swimming pool in my backyard right after having a hysterectomy. My world revolved around stuff. It didn't take long for me to feel the nag of being alone. I couldn't be alone; I had to find somebody. There was this new online dating thing happening, so I figured I would give that a whirl. That's where I met Christy. She was a police officer, and she lived eighty miles away. We partied together. I introduced her to my crowd, she introduced me to hers, and eventually, she left her job in her town, got a job at the Police Department near my city, and moved in with me.

I was working as a Transportation Manager, and I usually handled the hiring of all our drivers. But one day, while Christy and I were on vacation, my manager hired this new driver- Ray Navaroli. (Last name sound familiar?) He was a dependable driver but had the foulest mouth, worse than mine! And even though he was funny, he was also the biggest jerk. After we'd been working together for about a year, he confessed that he had a crush on me.

I said, "Dude, I'm gay."

To which he replied, "No, you're not. God didn't make you gay."

I said, "I don't know who your god is, but I was made gay."

So, for the next year, he'd always flirt with me. I'd tell him what a jerk he was for flirting with me since he had a girlfriend he was shacking up with and been for a while. (Talk about the pot calling the kettle black.) After a while, we kind of became friends, but I still thought he was the biggest jerk ever. One of my hardest workers—but a jerk.

I had no idea that I would be taking this guy's last name years down the road. But let's not get ahead of things just yet.

Chapter 26

Lightening Will Strike Any Minute Now

Now we've reached Easter Sunday 2011. And this is where we started in the introduction. I'm with my girlfriend Christy, and I had just given my life to God on the side of the road in my FedEx van. But the story isn't over because you don't just get saved, and *voila*, everything makes sense.

I didn't know how to pray, and I still didn't know who was talking to me. I hadn't broken up with Christy because my way of breaking up was cheating, and at that time, I was pretty sure if I touched any woman, I'd be struck by lightning, even if that woman happens to be my girlfriend of three years. That's the God I knew from the Bible. The God of fire and brimstone and 'going to hell.' I do not know about grace and mercy.

Now, something you need to understand about Christy is that she came from a Christian family. Her brother, Bubba, was a pastor, and her uncle was a pastor. She had a very close-knit family. They celebrated all the holidays and family occasions together- birthdays, weddings, etc. They were tight, tight.

But…there is no talk about homosexuality. Christy was a 39-year-old woman who had never been married, had no children, but always lived with roommates. Hello? They were from the Church of Christ denomination which meant they did not have any instruments in their worship. There would often be holiday gatherings where they would bust out with the hymnals and start singing. That would make me cringe with anger that I had to endure those songs. I would make an excuse for why I had to leave the room. They all treated me like family, but I was…just the roommate.

I had been planning Christy a 40th birthday party since before Easter. We had invited all our gay friends and ordered a keg. It was going to be a big bash to celebrate the big 4-0. The night of her birthday, the ladies I met at the Gretchen Wilson concert were there. Those two ladies and I stayed out by the pool until we floated the keg (emptied it dry). So, the next morning I was hungover with the worst headache imaginable. Here I was a month after I prayed that salvation prayer, and I thought my salvation was now voided because I got drunk. But I still didn't touch Christy because I had told him I had given him my lifestyle, and I didn't want to be zapped by lightning.

My love language is touch. I love to be touched and to touch. So, with all this no-touchy and distance between Christy and me, she began to wonder what was going on. I'm sure it weighed even heavier on her because a year before this, we had broken up for a brief moment. Even though we had broken up, she was still living in the house. However, during the break-up, I decided to visit Porterville for my 25th school reunion. While I was there, I hooked up for dinner with my old girlfriend. That same month, they were having a big gay pride parade in Dallas, so my old girlfriend came out to attend the parade with me.

Christy found out I had been with her and couldn't believe it. So now, a year later, here I am, being distant for no apparent reason to her. I'm trying to stay good on my own because I have no idea that God actually wants to help me along in the sanctification process. Heck, I don't even know what sanctification is! I don't even really know much about this God I gave my lifestyle over to. I'm listening to this radio station, and it is filling my heart, but there is still so much I don't know.

Chapter 27

Dear Christy,

$\mathcal{I}$ had been asking the voice, "How do I tell Christy. I know I need to tell her, but how do I do this?" On Saturday, June 5, 2011, at six in the morning, the voice woke me up. I brushed my head and said, "Really?" Like I'm shooing away a fly or something. "It's six in the morning, and I'm tired."

The voice said, "Write her a letter."

I threw back my blanket, peeved because I knew there wasn't any getting around this. I stomped out of bed and sat down at my laptop. "What do I write?"

"Tell her everything." He replied

So, I did.

Dear Christy,

It's 6:40 in the morning, and my mind will not turn off because my heart is filled with sadness, and my mind is in contemplation. But here it goes, if you really, really, really want to know what's been going on with me, here it goes. But first, I want you to be under-standing, open-minded, non-critical, or judgmental if possible.

Two months ago, while driving around Montgomery with end-less hours of time by myself, I started thinking about my life past and present, where I was today, how I got here, and so forth, and where my life would end. I was also becoming more open-minded to my mother's teachings about God (which none of it was about being gay, I promise), just what she was learning and bible people. It started not to sound too bad, after all the years that I had bashed it.

I had gotten to the point in that van that I would be so sick of the radio stations I was listening to. I started to channel surf; that's when I stumbled upon 107.1. It got my attention with the invest-ment program, but in that program, they talked about how God teaches us how to invest in the bible. I ignored that part because that wasn't my thing, but I figured if I could listen to the part about the money, I could deal with the rest. Well, there were times when I would leave my van, and when I got back, other preachers were on like Charles Stanley, David Lino, Michael Yousef, and others. It got to a point that I had the desire to listen to them as well and really found what they had to say very true and interesting.

The more I have listened, the more and more I want to go to heaven and be with God Almighty and be with my mom. I never used to care before. I thought that I could hide from God in this great big world, and he would just forget about this one little person amongst everyone else, and that was a lie that I let Satan tell me all my life. Christy, I do not want to stand before the throne of God to be judged. I would like to go straight to heaven because I did what was right and lived my life serving God. I know this sounds really corny from me, but that's why I have kept this a secret for so many months. If you can believe this, I even donated 5 bibles to a founda-tion called "Open Doors" that gets bibles overseas to countries that do not have them.

Christy, when I really got my eye-opener was when we watched "The Passion of the Christ" for Easter. Those eyes I couldn't get those eyes out of my mind for days. And when I was watching that movie, they kept saying, "I'm doing this for you." I started to wonder that someone has to love you so much that they were willing to go through that. And then I ask myself, "What have I done in appreciation for that sacrifice?" And the answer came back as "nothing." I lived my life the way I wanted and not given a damn about it. I have criticized Christianity and have made fun of my mother all these years, and condemned the church, and I have realized that I have been wrong all along. Jesus died for my sins, and I have come to learn and realize that I owe him my life.

So, then I started evaluating my life and what I could do to change it for the better. I pray every day and talk to God (I even pray for him to help stop cussing), and I have come to see the blessing that he has bestowed me. I listen to nothing but 107.1 all the time and not because I have to but because I want to. I really have come to enjoy the teaching, and I actually look forward to what I'm going to hear. So basically, I go to church every day. So usually, when I want to get off the phone, it's because I'm in the middle of a good teaching.

Christy, you are my best friend, but some months ago, without asking or praying for it, I lost the desire to be with any woman sexually. But I do not have the desire for a man either. I find myself right smack in the middle of asexual. I find it very confusing, but then again, I have chalked it up to being a God thing. So you have to know it is not you. God is way bigger than you. With that, I do believe that people are born gay. However, I am not one of those people. I was molested gay. I also had a traumatic event with Mike Madrid's death that was never dealt with properly. You know, all my life, my mom used to tell us, "tell me who you hang out with, and I'll tell you who you are" she was so right. I got involved with gay people, and that is where I got comfortable and settled in my life. This letter is not to tell you that I am going straight. That's not what this is. It's about where I want my soul to go for eternity, and you have to respect that. Going straight is not even a thought. I'm ok with asexual. You might think that all you have to be is a good person to get to heaven. Well, you might want to think again. I, however, am not going to take that chance. Vegas always wins, baby, and I am not going to gamble on this one.

Just to let you know, in all the time that I have been listening to the radio teachings, not once have I ever heard anything on homosexuality. And this is where my convictions come to play. I have given you and our relationship to God, and I told him to take this from me. And this was the hardest thing for me to do because I didn't want my best friend to go away if that is what he decides. But I have asked God to forgive me of all my sins, and that is why I have no physical contact with you. Not because I don't love you but because I know it's wrong. I'm not saying it's wrong for you, but it's wrong for me. I have been struggling with this for months now, and I can't let you suffer anymore with wondering what's going on with me. Someone whispered in my ear this morning and said, write it down. It's time. I'm believing it was God.

I love you
P.

I set the letter on the kitchen table so she would notice it when she got her morning cup of coffee. Christy knew my beliefs about God. They were non-existent. She read the letter, pushed it about arm's length, and said, "I can't compete with that. It looks like you need to go to church."

I looked at her and said, "Excuse me? I don't go to church." And she said, "No, but saved people do."

I hadn't been to church since I was a little girl. I asked her if they still wore dresses because, by this time, I had tattoos on my legs. She told me no, they wore jeans now.

After Christy pushed the letter aside, I put it in the filing cabinet and forgot about it until last year when I felt I need to write this book. It's interesting how God has you hang on to things for a later purpose sometimes.

While coming clean with Christy brought relief, it also brought a new set of unknowns. I had no idea how spiritually dehydrated I was. I would listen to that Christian radio station 12 hours a day, five days a week for three months. Something had dropped into my spirit, and I literally could not get enough. It was like when Jesus asked the woman at the well, "Do you thirst?"

I was like a dry sponge sucking up every ounce of water I could get. I remembered delivering packages to Lone Star Cowboy Church. Since Christy had said I needed to go to church, I thought maybe I would try that one out. Surely, they wore jeans since it was a cowboy church. I asked Christy if she would go with me, and she said she would.

Chapter 28

I Give It All to You

When we went to church the next day, I was N-E-R-V-O-U-S. I just knew I had the biggest L on my forehead. It could probably be seen for miles away, and they were going to kick us out because of it. My knees were shaking, and my hands were trembling. We sat in the very last row, and when the pastor made the salvation call asking if anyone wanted to receive salvation, I wanted to raise my hand, but Christy was right next to me. See, I still believed I had voided my salvation that night I got drunk at Christy's birthday bash, so I thought I had to do it again. Then I heard the voice, "Shame me in front of others, and I'll shame you in front of the Father."

My hand sprang up. But then the pastor said, "Ok, I want all of you who raised your hand to come down to the front."

I thought, "Oh no, please don't."

But the voice said, "Get up."

So, I moved. That aisle was longer than the hallway on The Shining. It seemed like it went on forever. I walked all the way to the front and said the sinner's prayer officially in front of a congregation and made my salvation known. Tears were falling down my face. They told us to see the altar team people. I met Rommie, and he prayed with me, talked with me for a few minutes, and invited me back.

I left the church that day, went home, and deleted every gay person off my Facebook and phone. I think I was left with ten contacts and thirty friends on Facebook who were straight. I told Christy she had to move into one of the spare bedrooms. She could live there as long as she needed to, as long as she wanted to. But she was going to be my friend, and that's all she was going to be. There would be no more sleeping together and no more relationship like that.

She went to church with me a few times because she liked the band and the music. But after those few times, she never went to church with me again because she was mad at me. I had followed through with what I had said in the letter. She realized I was serious about the change I was seeking. She said my conviction and my salvation made her question her lifestyle, and she was ticked off about it. She never went to church with me again.

That day I had also asked God, "Will you please take the drink?"

Today I have been sober for nine and a half years—no AA, I don't need a 12-step program. I have my one-step program, and His name is Jesus. No more drinking and partying. My Gretchen Wilson concert friends called me up to go party with them, and I told them I couldn't. I received Jesus as my Savior, and I'm going to church now.

They said, "Well, us and God, we have our own thing."

I didn't think I knew how to pray, but I would constantly talk to the voice out loud as I was driving around delivering packages. I said, "Look, you called me, you came after me, and now I have no friends. What am I going to do? I'm just by myself with me, you, and the radio. What am I going to do?"

I began to get very specific in these conversations, "Will you give me straight, heterosexual friends?" That was my prayer.

I had heard of a women's bible study at the church. I met some ladies in that group and even saw them on Sunday mornings and Wednesday night, but I still didn't have that friend connection with anyone. I still felt uncomfortable because of the scarlet L on my forehead, which I was sure everyone could see.

Then, one day as I was driving along, I heard the voice say, "Leave this person your number."

Well, 'this person' was a nice lady that was on my delivery route. Typically, I would type in the gate code and drop the package off in the barn. December before I got saved was the first time I had actually seen this woman. She smiled and asked if I would be in the area later. Because if I was, I was welcome to join her and her friends for tea and finger foods. I wrote it off as a weird thing and never joined them. Who invites their delivery person for tea?

Here I was having conversations with God about how uncomfortable I felt with these nice ladies at church, and here he was telling me to go and talk to the tea lady. It should have been a lightbulb moment, but I was looking for my answer in other places, not with the tea lady.

Just like before, I knew there was no getting around what the voice was telling me to do, so I might as well give in and get it over with because I knew he was persistent. I didn't have any packages to deliver this particular day, so I wrote my number down on one of those 'sorry we missed you' notes and stuck it to the keypad on the gate. The next thing I know, this woman is standing at the barn waving me in. I waved and tried yelling that I didn't have anything, but she is still waving me in. Oh, my gosh, this is so embarrassing.

I put in the code on the keypad and drove through. This woman had this big smile on her face, "What do you have for me?"

"Nothing."

Her eyebrow went up. "Nothing?"

I'm stammering about trying to figure out what to tell this woman, and the words just spill out of my mouth, "By any chance, are you a Christian?"

She hollers at her husband to come over. About this time, I am really regretting my decision to leave a note. I thought, *Oh, dear, she's going to kick me off her property.* But she looked at her husband and said, "This lady wants to know if I'm a Christian."

He smiled big, "Of course we are."

I released a huge sigh of relief; they weren't going to kick me off their property. Then I went on to tell them, "I just got saved a few months ago, and I've been praying for friends, and God told me to put my number on your keypad." Both she and her husband prayed over me right there on the spot.

Shar became my friend.

Chapter 29

Acts of Grace

Every time I went to church for a whole year, tears would flow out of my face like a waterfall during worship. It was like I was getting cleansed, and there was a lot for God to wash out. Even though I wanted friends, I still kept my distance from church people because I was still leery. They might think I was a nice lady, but what would they say if they ever discovered my past?

On Sunday, a couple of months after I walked down the aisle to "renew" my salvation, they announced they were having a newcomer luncheon, so I decided I would go, learn about the church and meet some people there. That day, I met Randy and Darla—the lead pastors and serval of the other pastors. They talked about how the church started and gave a little history of the church. They began listing off various ministries offered through the church, and one of them caught my attention. It was called *Caught in the Act of Grace* by Darla Weaver.

The Acts of Grace bible study focuses on healing women who have been sexually abused or gone through an abortion. I thought, *Are you kidding me? They talk about this stuff here?* I signed up for the sexual abuse course. I had no feelings or thoughts regarding my abortion, so signing up for that class never even crossed my mind. I told the Lord, "I'm going to sign up for this class, and if this doesn't help me, nothing will because I am tired of trying to fix that." At this point, I had already spent a lot of time and money seeking help from secular counselors.

The week before the class, I was nervous and anxious. When it finally got to the day of the study, I began prepping myself while I was getting ready, "Ok, I'm just going to stick to the basics, and that's it."

As I was driving to the class, I heard this voice say, "You don't need this class. You know that you will never be able, to be honest with everything you have been through or everything that you have done."

I had never heard this voice before, but it was undoubtedly correct. So, I turned around and headed back to the house. But then I heard the other voice, and I knew that voice. This voice said, "Go. You need to go."

Because of my hesitation and circling about, when I arrived at the class, everyone had already chosen their seats, and the only one left was right next to the leader. I knew it was the leader's spot because all the material was stacked next to it. The setting took me back to my kindergarten years. I was mortified and wanted to bolt. Even more so when the leader walked into the room, it was the lead pastor, Darla! Eight people in this room, including me, and all I can think about is my escape plan. That other voice I didn't recognize said, "You'll never be able, to be honest now. Not with her here. This isn't working, and you're done."

I thought *You're right. I'll leave at lunch.*

Darla stood up and said, "Let's pray." We all stood in a circle holding hands like a real kumbaya church prayer. Since I was so nervous, my hands were sweating like crazy! When she finished the prayer, she wiped the hand that had been holding mine on the side of her pants as she said, "My goodness, it's going to be ok."

Now I'm embarrassed because all the attention is on me. But it faded as we jumped into the guidelines for the course. One of the guidelines stated: If I ever decide to leave this group, I will have to come back and tell the group why I left because my presence will be missed.

Are you kidding me? I have to explain if I want to leave?

As I'm toying with this thought, Darla started a video. A little girl in a white dress is running through the woods with a red rose. She looks back and drops the rose. A man's legs start walking toward the girl, he steps on the rose, and I start freaking out because I know this little girl is about to get molested. The screen goes black for a brief moment, and on comes Darla giving her testimony.

She begins talking about being sexually abused as a child, having an abortion, and being raped a couple of times because of the life she was living. As I hear all this, her transparency allowed me to take a breath and think, "Ok, I guess it's ok for me to talk. She went through all of this, and she is a pastor and a pastor's wife."

I was good until we opened the book "Caught in the Acts of Grace." The turmoil intensified with every page we turned. I'm pretty sure they were taking bets that I wouldn't come back after the lunch break. But I went back. September 25, 2011- right in the middle of the course, I decided to get baptized. I called my mom and told her I had gotten saved. She was so thankful the Lord had answered her prayers. My mom flew in, and Tammy and my nieces came as well. My nieces had only known me as gay their entire lives, so this was freaking them out. Christy even came.

I remember popping out of the water and seeing tears streaming down Christy's face. She knew at that moment there was no turning back. She knew she had to face that this was permanent. And after that, things changed around the house once again. She became even more resentful of me, and we were constantly on edge with each other.

In October, the church had a huge event called West Fest. I still didn't have what I would consider friends at the church, but I did enjoy being around the women from my Acts of Grace class. I could at least relate to the things they'd endured and were working through like me. We had a common ground of respect for each other like comrades in arms.

I was walking around by myself when Darla walked up to me and gave me a hug. She put her arm through mine and said, "Walk with me."

As we walked around, I thought, "Woman, what are people going to think when they find out I'm an ex-lesbian? You probably shouldn't even be associating yourself with me."

But Darla didn't care; she loved me with the love of Christ. And when Christy showed up after work and I introduced them, she showed her the same kind of love with a smile on her face as she said, "Nice to meet you."

No judgment. Darla's actions that night sealed the deal for me on this God thing. She did not judge my ex-girlfriend or me. She treated us with dignity and respect, and that meant something to me. I now felt like I could continue going to that church without any ugliness towards me, without anything hanging over me or holding me back.

That was the last event Christy ever went to church with me.

At the end of Acts of Grace, I had started walking into my healing. I began realizing and admitting to myself that I wasn't born gay. Satan constantly contradicts the truth and said, "Yes, you were." He'll always bring you back to those lies.

But while I was attending the course, the truth settled into my heart. I was not born gay, it was a lifestyle I chose for myself, and now, all these years later, I was dealing with the consequences of that choice. I had never been married, I had never had children, and I would never have any grandchildren.

Acts of Grace had a second class for women who had an abortion. I had told Darla I didn't need to attend that class, but she insisted, so I went. At the beginning of the course, they give you an hour to sit by yourself and write out your story. It was during this time I remembered the nurse telling me to go through with the abortion and telling me it was a girl. I had completely blocked all that out. With that memory came a flood of grief. I had never grieved over the loss of my child. I just stuffed it and drank it away. On the way home, I went out to this little peninsula on the lake. There was nobody out there, so I fell to my knees and bawled. I don't know how long I cried and told my baby I was sorry I had killed her.

All my life, people had asked if I had any kids; I had always told them, no, but that was a lie. I had a daughter. Later on, when I taught Acts of Grace in prison, I would tell those inmates that I should be in a jumpsuit with them. I had murdered my child; I just did it legally.

There is not a person on this planet who doesn't have skeletons. We can't hide anything from God. We've got to dig through everything and come to Him raw. Going through the sexual abuse and abortion classes was not easy, but they were necessary for me to grow. One of my favorite stories in the Bible is Mary when she came and broke her alabaster box before the Lord. That was the ultimate worship service in the Bible; it doesn't get any better than that. It was the rawest moment in her life. She took everything she had, broke it before him, and everything poured out. We must break like that box and allow everything to pour out.

A lot of people live by the lie, "If I don't talk about it, it didn't happen." Many people think they might be rejected if they tell the truth. God wants us to fully disclose everything to Him so He can help us and heal us.

Sometimes we won't allow ourselves to heal due to resistance. It doesn't feel good to heal. I've had several surgeries, and none of them felt good to heal. But here I am years after those surgeries; I have scars, I remember the process, I remember what happened, but I don't remember the pain. That's how healing is. Or should be.

Chapter 30

Thou Art Loosed!

Ray Navaroli and I had worked together at two different companies together, and every once in a while, he would call me up just to chat. He always called me P, never Priscilla. In one of these conversations, I mentioned that I was now saved. He said, "Oh does that mean you're not gay anymore?"

I said, "No, it just means I am me."

He said, "Oh, you want to go to church?"

Go to church? This was coming from the biggest loudmouth I knew. The guy who'd sit in his office screaming at his girlfriend on the phone while I looked at Penny, the receptionist, and said, "How would you like to be married to that jerk?"

I just laughed at Ray and said, "That mouth doesn't go to church."

Ray was an East Coast Italian and cussed way more than I did. And I thought I had a foul mouth. Cussing was something I had asked God to take away from me, so it would gong around in my head whenever I would cuss.

One day, he called me up and asked if I had ever been to a *Woman, Thou Art Loosed* conference. He told me TD Jakes was putting it on, and I would love it. Then he said he would pick me up and drive me to Houston for the conference. He wouldn't be able to stay because it was only for women.

So, he drove about an hour to my house to pick me up, another hour to the conference, and then came back to pick me up and take me home. It was quite the grand gesture from someone who I thought was godless. But I didn't think much of it at the time. I had never been to an event like this, so I had no idea what I was getting myself into. He handed me $60 and said, "Here's some money; go ahead and buy yourself whatever you want."

He told me they had merchandise I'd be able to purchase. I walked into this conference, and there were booths with merchandise just as Ray had said there would be. I was by myself clueless as to what all this stuff was. This event had about 16,000 African American women in attendance. I'm pretty sure I was only part of a handful of white women in there. As I walk around to these booths with merchandise, I had no idea what I should be looking for or what I should buy. But I heard the voice say, "Stop." So that is the booth where I stopped. I looked at the merchandise laid out then asked the lady running the booth if this Sheryl Brady was any good.

She said, "Oh my gosh, yes, have you never heard of her?"

I bought some of her DVDs and walked into the auditorium for the event. My seat was up in the nosebleeds since Ray had purchased it last minute, but I was excited to be present. They started worshiping, and I had never felt the Holy Ghost like I felt Him at that moment. He was swirling, just swirling. I had tears running down my face. After worship, they invite their first speaker up, who just so happened to be Pastor Sheryl Brady from The Potters House North Dallas.

I was like, "Oh, I have her DVDs." I'm going to figure out what she is all about. She started to preach, and her message that night hit home to every point of my life. I was heaving bawling. I felt the shame, guilt, and worthlessness falling off of me. When they say, "Woman, thou art loosed," that's precisely what happened to me that day.

This little black lady in her late 70's was standing next to me; she put her arm around me and hugged me, "It's ok baby, everything's gonna be all right."

I left that conference on Cloud 9. Ray picked me up, and I could not wait to get home and watch those DVDs. I watched them over and over, then I bought some more and watched those over and over. Sheryl Brady became my first spiritual mentor, and she didn't even know my name! Only God knows how she ministered to me. I have accumulated over 130 of her sermons, and each one has spoken into my life. I grew exponentially in my walk with the Lord listening to all her sermons.

"So then faith comes by hearing, and hearing by the word of God." Romans 10:17

Chapter 31

Prison? What?

Not long into my salvation, I kept hearing the word 'prison.' I had no idea why I kept hearing this. Like, prison. What? Marco? Polo? I told the ladies in my Acts of Grace class that "I keep hearing the word prison." I didn't know why I kept hearing it, and I wanted some answers. They didn't have any but suggest that God could be calling me to do prison ministry. I started to think about, is God calling me into prison ministry? I've never been to prison, so that'd be weird. I opened my laptop and typed in prison ministries near me. He didn't give me direction; he just gave me a word. I found all these prison ministries. None of them were in my town. I closed my laptop and didn't know what to do with that.

In January 2012, Ray asked me if I would go to church with him AGAIN. Since he was now asking almost every week, I said ok. I told him to meet me at David Lino's church. He was one of the radio pastors I enjoyed listening to every weekday. He asked if he could pick me up, but I said no, it's not a date.

When I walked into the church, they handed me one of those 'What's Happening in Our Church' flyers. I opened it up, and the first thing I saw was: Women's Prison Ministry. I said,

"Well, that is nice, God, but I am not in Kingwood at 5 pm on that day of the week to leave with them. I am an hour and a half away delivering packages in Montgomery in my FedEx truck." And I left it at that.

In March of 2012, I received a phone call from an old work colleague. He said, "Hey Priscilla, I want to see if you would be willing to come work for us as our dispatch manager."

It sounded like a great opportunity that would provide me with a little more money. So, I had someone manage my FedEx routes and took the job. And do you know what happened to be right across the street from my new office? The church with the prison ministry! It was one of those moments you look up to the sky and go, "Oh, looks like you figured it out."

I went to the church and told them I was interested in the prison ministry. They introduced me to the lady in charge of it, and I met with Anna for coffee. The prison they went to was an hour and a half away from my house, Plane State Prison for Women. As soon as I walked in there, I fell in love with it. I would go straight from work, meet them in the parking lot and ride with them to the prison. The class started at 6:30 or seven, and we wouldn't leave the prison until 8:30. Which meant every Tuesday night for six months, I didn't get back home until 10. It was my most anticipated day of the week.

When I began working with the ministry, I had only been saved less than a year and didn't know the bible very well. The other ladies were well versed in their bible. For this reason, I never got to lead anything. My duty was to give the inmates a piece of paper, a pencil, and a hug. It didn't matter much to me. I enjoyed being there. There were times when one of the prisoners would say, "I don't understand why it's wrong to be gay."

Those little Baptist ladies, Anna and Georgina, who led the ministry would turn to me. I'd think, *Oh, now I get to talk, sweet.* Then I'd begin talking with the women about my testimony and what God had shown me in my own life. They couldn't combat me like they could combat the others. It felt like a Saul to Paul conversion. Ladies, this is how I used to think, but my eyes have been opened to a new way of thinking, a new way of living.

Around this same time, Ray began telling me his testimony. He told me he had received a 25-year prison sentence but got out after ten years because his mother hired a lawyer who got him parole. I said, "Oh, you're a thug?"

To which he replied, "You're not right."

As I mentioned before, Ray had some weird crazy crush on me. We had stayed in touch even though we no longer worked together, but we began chatting a lot more. Somewhere in those casual conversations, I had told him, "If I ever think of dating a guy, he'll have to be a Godly man."

I suppose that impacted his decision-making because he started going to the church we had visited together and attended their men's study group. He rededicated his life to the Lord and began transforming right before my eyes. Eventually, around the summer of 2012, we started dating. Ray always told me he was my diamond in the dirt. Little did I know how right he would be.

Chapter 32

Learning Christianize

After I got saved and had been going to church for several weeks, I got the courage to walk into a Christian bookstore for the very first time. I had never in my life been in a bible bookstore. I was amazed at all the little knick-knacks, CDs, bibles, and books from all these authors. I went to the Bible section, and that's where the confusion began. As I stared at this huge section, I wondered, "NASB? NLT? NIV? What is all this stuff?"

I was so out of my element I had no idea where to begin, and I really didn't want to ask these Christian people for help. They didn't need to know I was a newbie who knew nothing. So, I decided to buy another book that day, *Bibles for Dummies*.

As an outsider coming in, Christians have no idea how confusing all their lingo is because they've heard it so often it is now common knowledge. But seriously, "if you want to be white as snow, you have to get washed in the blood of the Lamb?" If that isn't a perfect example of an oxymoron, I don't know what would be. I knew I didn't know stuff. My problem was not being sure who to confide in with my ignorance.

When I was in the gay community, coming out wasn't as accepted as it is today. So, we'd have a few insider things we'd ask to confirm our suspicions about others. We might say, "Are you family?" or "Are you P-L-U (people like us)?" If they had no clue what we were talking about, we knew they were straight. Christians didn't' have this simplicity. I felt like I was trying to learn a foreign language at times. And even sometimes, a bit like Chris Rock from Rush Hour, "No one understands the words that are coming out of your mouth." Like, "Hey, preacher, I'm really trying here, but…what?!"

While I was in the bookstore, some ladies were talking about the Trinity. I had no idea what they were talking about, so I felt embarrassed and insecure. It wasn't until I heard a sermon on the radio about the Trinity–Father, Son, Holy Spirit – that I finally understood. Those radio programs taught me a lot, but I knew I would have to bite the bullet and get my own Bible. So, I went back to the Christian bookstore; told the clerk I was buying my first Bible. She was so excited and so sweet. She got me an NKJV and kind of explained how to use it. She convinced me to buy the little tabs to put on the pages to find where the books were. Those were helpful.

Then came the decision I knew that I'd have to make. I was either going to believe all the Bible or none of it. But it wasn't going to be half-true; there was going to be no picking and choosing for me. Which meant the first thing I needed to take care of was finding out what it said about being gay. I started in Genesis, God created man in His image, and he made Adam and Eve, and they were to become fruitful and multiply. Ok. I didn't go to Sodom and Gomorrah because that was a story they always flung at gays. But I soon found myself in 1 Corinthians 6.

"Do you not know that the unrighteous will not inherit the kingdom of God? Do not be deceived. Neither fornicators, nor idolaters, nor adulterers,

*nor homosexuals, nor sodomites, nor thieves, nor
covetous, nor drunkards, nor revilers, nor extor-
tioners will inherit the kingdom of God. And such
were some of you. But you were washed, but you
were sanctified, but you were justified in the name
of the Lord Jesus and by the Spirit of our God." 1
Corinthians 6:9&10 (NKJV)*

Verse 11 had the best news ever! *"And such were some of you."*
Paul was talking to the church here, which meant I wasn't the
only wretch out there who had been *washed, sanctified, and justified in the name of the Lord Jesus.* Woo who! I didn't have to
worry about the big L on my forehead any longer!

*"Therefore God also gave them up to uncleanness,
in the lusts of their hearts, to dishonor their bodies
among themselves, who exchanged the truth of
God for the lie, and worshiped and served the crea-
ture rather than the Creator, who is blessed forever. Amen.*

*For this reason God gave them up to vile passions.
For even their women exchanged the natural use
for what is against nature. Likewise also the men,
leaving the natural use of the woman, burned in
their lust for one another, men with men committing what is shameful, and receiving in themselves
the penalty of their error which was due.*

*And even as they did not like to retain God in their
knowledge, God gave them over to a debased mind,
to do those things which are not fitting; being
filled with all unrighteousness, sexual immorality,
wickedness, covetousness, maliciousness; full of
envy, murder, strife, deceit, evil-mindedness; they*

are whisperers, backbiters, haters of God, violent, proud, boasters, inventors of evil things, disobedient to parents, undiscerning, untrustworthy, unloving, unforgiving, unmerciful; who, knowing the righteous judgment of God, that those who practice such things are deserving of death, not only do the same but also approve of those who practice them." Romans 1:24-32 NKJV

So many years of my life, Christians had thrown what was said to be the Word of God at me, "You're gay, you're going to hell." But now, I was reading the words for myself, and my own eyes were open. God wasn't gay bashing! He was addressing all people, even the straight ones! Fornicators and those committing adultery? I knew some of them! Here it was in black and white. God's plan for sex was for a husband and wife who had committed to each other through the covenant of marriage. Period. It was about living differently from the world.

I had already been broken up with Christy for four or five months, but it was at that very moment, I decided I would never have sex again until I got married, or if I never got married, then I would never have sex again. God designed it this way, and if I was to honor Him with my life, this was what I had to do. I started reading my Bible, but not very much. I was trying to read it like a book, and the Bible isn't meant to be read like a book.

Chapter 33

Resist & Flee 101

*I*n December of 2011, I was praying for a best friend. At the same time, I considered Shar, and her husband Butch, to be friends; I just didn't do things with them. We'd visit every once in a while, but they weren't people I would randomly grab lunch with but would only visit them at their home. I knew the ladies in the Acts of Grace class, but I didn't have friends I hung out with regularly. I wanted a best friend, someone I could hang out with.

As I was finishing up my Acts of Grace class, I was contacted by someone at the church asking if I would like to join some of the church members for an event. I thought that sounded like an excellent opportunity to get out of the house, so I met them in the church parking lot on the scheduled night. I've mentioned before that I felt like I had a big L on my forehead whenever I was around church people. One of the reasons I felt this way is because of the casual conversation starters they would always lead with, "So, are you married? Do you have any kids?" You get the strange look when you're 45 and have never been married or had any kids. What's wrong with you? During the event, I met a woman; she was pleasant to me. We began talking, and before I knew it, we became friends. I've only been a Christian, not quite a year, and I have no roots. I don't know anything about this *roaring lion seeking who he might devour*. (1 Peter 5:8) So talking to a co-worker who was also a gay minister kind of threw a wrench in my mind. I'm sitting here trying to sort out four decades of lies when she comes along and says, "It's ok to be a Christian and be gay."

Dear Christians, maybe the first lesson for new Christians should be about wolves in sheep's clothing and not being deceived. Just a thought here. I was not prepared at all. She's telling me being gay is ok, and I'm beginning to question what I believe. My fleshly desires are still there, but I had planned to hand those over to God and pick up His way of living. Was I incorrect in thinking I had to do that? Was I mistaken in thinking He wanted me to do that? Maybe God loved me enough to let me do what I wanted to? Man, it was all so confusing.

That's when the emails and text messages began. Right in the middle of the confusion, right when I was most vulnerable. I wasn't praying every day; I wasn't daily reading my Bible. I was like a sheep walking straight to the slaughter. The first tiny seed Satan planted was a text message from this church lady with her testimony. It casually mentioned she had been married a couple of times and had also been involved with women sexually. I looked at it and didn't overthink it, "Really? I wouldn't have guessed." Little did I know it would be just the opening of a colossal floodgate.

About a month later, she sends me an email, and somewhere in the middle of the email, she starts telling me that she has been fanaticizing about me while she's having sexual relations with her husband.

Have you ever heard of spiritual warfare or oppression? Yeah, I hadn't heard of any of that. By this time, I was dating Ray. But on the other side of the coin, I have a gay pastor at work telling me it is ok to be a gay Christian and someone at my church telling me about lesbian fantasies with me. I seriously wish I had made this up. I began feeling like I was drowning. I felt something clawing the back of my neck and pulling me down. I replied to the email via text and said, "That was interesting." Then I never brought it up again.

Even though I didn't know all these spiritual things were happening, I knew something was not right. I went to Shar and asked her to pray for me because I was having lesbian desires again. She prayed and spoke in tongues, casting out Satan, but nothing helped. Ray and I were now starting to bicker and argue because I'm not being very nice to him. Now that these lesbian thoughts were floating through my mind, he didn't stand a chance. I was still uncomfortable with a man touching me. I'd freak out when he held my hand or touched my back. And now, I'm questioning if my old relationship habits were acceptable. If they were, why was I wasting time being so uncomfortable with Ray?

Even my dreams became tainted with lesbian fantasies. It was like an Armageddon happening in my soul; problems with Ray, weird messages from this church lady, the gay preacher saying it is all good. I could feel myself slipping towards my old lifestyle, and I felt like I had no way of escaping the slide. I told God he had to save me, but I had no idea what was pulling me.

In the middle of June 2012, on a Monday night, I had this dream that a woman came to me. It was a sexual dream, and I told her I couldn't be with her because I didn't want to grieve the Holy Spirit. Tuesday night, I had another dream, same scenario, same situation, but this time I caved in. In this dream, while I was in the middle of this sexual relationship, I looked at God and said, "I'm sorry, but I need to take care of me."

I woke up the next morning and bawled my eyes out. I said I know I didn't do it, but I'm so sorry. I called Pastor Darla and asked her to pray for me. She told me I had to combat Satan even in my dreams; pray before you go to sleep. I asked her to pray for me again at church, and I was feeling a little better.

God knows I don't want it, but I'm battling something I've lived for 30 years.

This lady and I actually become friends. Then, along comes the Fourth of July. I went to her house for a barbeque with her and her husband. It was getting late, and she suggested I could stay the night. I didn't think anything of it and happily agreed to sleep in the spare bedroom. Her husband went to sleep in the master bedroom, and she came to stay with me in the spare bedroom. I figured it was a common thing. It was not a common thing! I could feel the energy in that room. If I had known the story of Joseph and Potiphar's wife, I would have known this would be the perfect time to FLEE! But I had no such knowledge at the time. It was like there was an audience waiting to see what was about to happen. Here was my dream coming into play right at this moment. We started making out, that's all we did, but I immediately felt God turn his back on me and the flame went out. Not that He forsook me, but He couldn't look at the sin that was taking place. I went home the next day, and the feeling of separation between God and me was awful. I called her and asked if she felt guilty. She said, "For what? We didn't do anything wrong."

My mind was about to explode. "What do you mean? We just made out homosexually not to mention the adultery!"

She replied, "It's two women; it doesn't make a difference."

I didn't know what to do, so I went to the only person I knew to talk to about it—my gay pastor co-worker. I saw the church counselor at Lone Star weekly, but I didn't want to tell her. After all, my friend was very involved with the church. The counselor would probably think it was me who started everything. At least that's what I thought would happen, so that fear kept me away from the one place I probably would have received help.

Instead, I went to the gay pastor, who told me I didn't do anything wrong. If that was the case, why didn't it sit well with my spirit? I felt Godly remorse. I felt like I needed to repent. I tried to do this with my friend and the gay pastor, but neither would accept I had done anything in need of repentance. I told God I was so sorry, but it continued to hang on me and weigh me down more and more. If only I had heard Peter's instructions:

> *"Therefore gird up the loins of your mind, be sober, and rest your hope fully upon the grace that is to be brought to you at the revelation of Jesus Christ; as obedient children, not conforming yourselves to the former lusts, as in your ignorance; but as He who called you is holy, you also be holy in all your conduct, because it is written, "Be holy, for I am holy.""* 1 Peter 1:13-16 (NLT)

Chapter 34

But I Must Confess

It took me two months to muster up the courage of doing the brave thing. I asked to speak with the church counselor and Pastor Darla. I had never even heard the verse that says confess your sins to one another, but the Holy Spirit was compelling me to do this. And it was necessary for me if I wanted to continue in my Christian walk. I scheduled the meeting and signed a waiver stating Darla could be present. I sat down and looked at them. There wasn't any way to soften it or fluff it up, so I told them what I had done and what we had done. I thought Darla's vein was going to pop out of her head. I thought, at that moment, she was angry at me, but that was far from the truth. Darla had just found out someone she trusted had done this.

I personally took all the blame upon myself because I was the one who walked in with the L on my forehead. I thought they were blaming me not realizing what was actually going on. I hadn't initiated any of this. The church lady had abused her leadership position. She was required to step down, tell her husband the truth and attend marriage counseling. She refused. Why would she need counseling when she was in denial of the issue? It was like me attending an AA meeting, "Why do I need to be taught how to get rid of this? I've got it under control."

During the summer, Ray and I had gotten engaged. It was right in the middle of all this lesbian chaos. My final attempt to chase away the lifestyle. I broke off the engagement in October and told him, "I don't want to be with anybody, no female, no male, nothing."

I had asked God for forgiveness, but I didn't know how to "walk in repentance." I even went and apologized to my friend's husband face to face asking for his forgiveness. We still had a friendship for a little while, which made things kind of awkward attending Lone Star. So, for a few Sundays, I decided to attend this Holy Roller Pentecostal church. People were dancing and running around the room, which made it easy for me to kneel at the alter unnoticed, bawling my eyes out. I repented as much as I repented in the FedEx truck the first day, and I gave things over to God. But this time, I was sad because I had betrayed the Holy Spirit. I had been too weak to fight my own flesh.

Somewhere in October, Darla asked me to go to Angola State Penitentiary in Louisiana. We stayed on the grounds as the warden's guest for three nights. On the way back, I asked if she would be my one-on-one mentor. I knew the importance of a sponsor from my AA days. She said she would. During this time, she realized I was still hanging out with the church lady. She hadn't realized how much we were hanging out, and she nearly blew her lid even though it was merely platonic. She said either I stop hanging out with my friend, or she would stop mentoring me- I had to choose.

By this time, my friend threw me under the bus and blamed me for everything. But I had the email! I gave it to Darla and the counselor. In December 2012, our friendship ended because I chose to be mentored, I chose to grow, I chose Jesus.

When I cried out to the Lord and told him what I had done, I felt the oppression lift. That clawing on my back, the drowning feeling, they left with my confession. I haven't had another thought of a woman since. The reason I had found myself in this place was that I hadn't been prepared. I was coasting by doing the bare minimum, unaware of the training I needed to equip myself for this war.

I began getting up to read my bible before I went to work, 4:30 every morning! Under Darla's mentorship, I began to learn about prayer, healthy boundaries, growing in the Lord, making wise decisions, and so forth. The Holy Spirit spoke clearly to me, "Now you see what Satan is capable of; you are not exempt."

Wow. It was so true. I had thought I could approach this like anything else in my life—depend entirely on myself. But God doesn't work that way. He wants dependency on Him. I had to meditate on Him and His ways if I wanted my life to change. When I became a leader in the Acts of Grace ministry, I always told my ladies, "You're only as sick as your secrets."

It's those hidden things that will get you every time. The things that we don't want to talk about are the very things we need to expose so we can face the truth and allow accountability.

"And now, dear brothers and sisters, one final thing. Fix your thoughts on what is true, and honorable, and right, and pure, and lovely, and admirable. Think about things that are excellent and worthy of praise. Keep putting into practice all you learned and received from me—everything you heard from me and saw me doing. Then the God of peace will be with you." Philippians 4:8&9 (NLT)

From that moment on, I wouldn't allow myself ten seconds to linger on a thought that was against God's standards. When they came at me, I would start thinking about what His word said. I trained myself to think about "these things."

Let's be practical; if you suddenly think of a slice of pizza or a nice big steak, what happens when you let that thought linger? It doesn't go away on its own. It begins to invade your entire body. Suddenly, your mouth begins to salivate. Your body even begins to plead its case, "If we can just have this, we will be satisfied."

Feed your spirit! If I had a dream, I would wake up and immediately say, "Not today Satan." I'd forget about the dream and not even think about it. I wanted no part of it. That is how we need to treat ungodliness. Our flesh will try its best to convince us that it is just one...bite, drink, kiss, or look—just one. But we have to remember, if we're walking on a narrow ledge, one step can be a matter of life or life-altering consequences.

After that awful ungodly act in my life, I started my morning with this prayer, a prayer I continue to this day:

Melt me of who I am

Mold me into what You want me to be

Fill me with what You want me to have, and

Use me in the way You want to use me

It changed my life, submit to Him, and I promise you won't be disappointed. That's not to say there won't be others who bring disappointment into your life. Looking back, I could have easily walked away from the church and God after my friend threw me under the bus. After all, hypocrisy was the biggest fault I saw in the church, mainly my mother, throughout my life. I believe the only reason it didn't trip me up this time was that, for once, I was more focused on God than the faults of others.

> *"So now that you know God (or should I say, now that God knows you), why do you want to go back again and become slaves once more to the weak and useless spiritual principles of this world?"*
> *Galatians 4:9 (NLT)*

Chapter 35

I Want You to Feel Special

Since I ended the last chapter speaking about the faults of others, I thought this would be a great opportunity to take a moment to talk about my mom. I know I've talked a lot about the wrong things my mom took us through: moving like we were running from the law, crappy relationships, hypocrisy, and so on. I'm sure every one of us can look back and find moments where our parents' decisions paved the way for at least a few sessions of counseling.

But I want to take a moment to reflect on some of my mom's good qualities that also impacted my life. Before I got saved, it was easy for me to focus on every one of her shortcomings in her life, mainly because I didn't want to own up to my faults. But after I got saved, I realized the process of sanctification could be quite messy. The easiest way to describe it is once you realize how much grace God gives you, it is easier to extend more grace to others.

For the record, I was my mom's favorite. You can ask any of my siblings; they still give me a hard time to this day. I'll say, "Oh, I think mom is upset with me."

And they will reply, "What? The golden child upset mom?"

But it's true. I remember when mom would take me after school, and we would get a sundae alone. She'd always tell me not to say anything to my siblings. Now that we are older, I've never asked them if she had done the same with them and told us the same thing, but those were precious moments.

Another amazing thing she did was to make sure each of us knew we were individuals and special. She did this by letting us each have our own TV Show. My show was Charlie's Angels, as I mentioned before. And I remember one of my brothers liking Mister Roger's Neighborhood. She always made sure that if we had our show, it was our time and moment. Nobody else was allowed to change the channel during our showtime. They could watch it with us or leave the room, but that was our time on the TV.

She loved giving us the desires of our heart, well, except for Dickey pants. But in all seriousness, my mom worked her butt off cleaning houses to ensure we were not lacking. Tammy was a dancer growing up, and I remember all the stuff she always needed. New ballet slipper, new toe shoes, tap dancing shoes, and of course, there were all the costumes for every recital. Mom would be up into the wee hours at the sewing machine. I was in sports for a time, and I needed cleats for track and field, softball equipment, and so on. My mom tried to put me in dance classes once, but that was a complete failure. Although, I'm sure there is still a photo out there with me in a tutu. Each one of my mom's seven kids had their gifts and talents, and she made darn sure that we never heard, "You can't be involved in that because we don't have the money." Instead, she would find another house to clean.

She always made sure the house was clean and used to tell us, "You may be poor, but you don't have to look like it."

Despite all the flaws the rebellious teenage in me could pick out, she had so many good qualities too. She loved us all so much. Another way she showed us love was by making each of our birthdays a special day. She'd ask us what we wanted her to make for dinner and what kind of cake we wanted every year.

Every birthday, I always asked for spaghetti. That was my absolute favorite meal. On top of all this, My mom has a special birthday song she sings to us. "How old are you, my pretty little miss? How old are you, my honey? I hear you say you're (we reply our age) (she repeats the age) years old this (she'd say the day of the week it is)." I am 54 years old, and I have heard that song 54 times. And as I sit here and write these words, I realize I will hear this song again next week, and maybe for the last time. I will be truly sad when mom goes home to be with the Lord, and I have to celebrate my birthday without hearing that sung to me, as I am sure the rest of my siblings will be as well. I am thankful that day has not yet come.

One of my favorite birthday memories came from the year I turned fourteen. I asked for spaghetti, no surprise there, but I also asked for a round champagne cake. Mom made up the spaghetti and got me the cake. I was so happy. Despite all the disagreements we had, she still made me feel special.

Chapter 36

Obedience, You said What?

The struggle to be obedient is the hard part with God. Give this person $20 that's easy; give this person a burger that's sitting on the corner, easy. Love that person not so easy. God will give us the easy things when we first start our journey to maturity, and then we will grow into the hard stuff as long as we show we'll be obedient. Go and do prison ministry, lead an Acts of Grace class, easy stuff. Marry Ray? God's done lost His mind! From one stubborn person to another, I'm going to clue you in- if you don't want to be obedient from the beginning, it will be a struggle all throughout your walk with Christ. Baptism after salvation is the first step in obedience. That is your first sign of obedience; if you refuse to do that, how will you obey when he asks you to do something else. As unsaved people, we are used to doing stuff our own way, so it takes time to learn to be submissive when we become saved. Yes, Jesus loves us, but he is also our Master and Lord. There comes a moment when we will have to decide if He's Lord of all or not Lord at all.

To be obedient is the decision I had to make when it came to Ray. Was God Lord of all of my life, or could I handle the relationship department on my own and do my own thing? I wasn't the only one bringing baggage to the table. Most people didn't know the Ray I had initially met. Yes, when we met, he knew Jesus, but he knew the prison Jesus version. He got saved in prison but immediately went back to his old ways once he left. Often, I saw that jerk. We were two stubborn, prideful, not willing to bend people that came in contact with a God who was trying to break each of us.

Initially, I started dating him because I was curious. I hadn't been with a woman in a year, and this man liked me, so I wondered if I could do this. I was also starting to regret that Satan had stolen so much from me: marriage, kids, grandchildren. He stole a whole family from me. In the past, I had never been able to feel comfortable around a man unless I was drunk, and even then, it still felt awkward. It was a roller coaster of emotions. He'd drive an hour and a half to come to see me. We'd get into an argument ten minutes into his visit, and he'd go an hour and a half back. We began meshing pretty well, but then the whole lesbian incident occurred with my friend from church, and that set us back.

I had told Darla that God told me to marry Ray, so every time I started getting cold feet, she would say, "Did God tell you to marry Ray?"

"Yes."

"Then be obedient."

Oh, if only it were that easy. We were engaged a month the first time before I broke things off, and then we got engaged again. This time, we decided to attend the Gettin' Hitched bible study at Lone Star. We dropped out of it twice. The first time we made it to week three and the second time, week five. One of the exercises asked us to list ten reasons we wanted to marry this person. I didn't have ten; I had one- God told me to. That was it! We attended our first Gettin' Hitched in 2012 when a few weeks later, I said to the leader, who was also the church counselor, I couldn't do it. I wasn't comfortable being in the class, so I would have to tell Ray I couldn't marry him. But before I walked away entirely, I asked if my being a lesbian for thirty years would have any bearing on my issues. She said, "Oh gosh, yes." From that day, this church counselor sat with me every Wednesday night at seven for two years. It was as if the Acts of Grace classes had penetrated the surface, but these sessions went down to the bone. We went through so many layers, reliving so many events; it was so painful and so good. I sat there for two years until one day; I was like, "I don't think I have anything else to talk about." I walked out of that counseling as a healed woman. Counseling is a great thing. We have to get outside of our old way of thinking. We can't do the same things over and over and expect different results; that's the definition of insanity

We ended up completing the Gettin' Hitched study in a one-on-one setting. When I finally let God do in me what I couldn't do for myself, I saw Ray in a different light. Ray eventually became my Kingsman redeemer, which is profound. I would get excited to see him, hold his hand, rub his hair, tell him I loved him. Because I told God he needed to put love for that man in me. And he did.

I know Abraham didn't want to take Isaac up that mountain. I'm sure he was shaking in his sandals. But the angel said, "Now I know you fear the Lord." Abraham did it out of obedience, and God showed up at the last minute. Split seconds. That's what God did for me with Ray. He didn't show up for me when we were dating or in the midst of all of that. He showed up for me before the wedding. Just months before the wedding. I'm planning, I've got my dress, and I'm still praying, "Help me, Lord." He showed up for me just a couple of months before. Then I fell in love with that man, and I loved Raymond Navaroli Jr.

Don't think for a moment that God telling me to marry Ray somehow miraculously made everything wonderful. That first year of marriage was a huge struggle. I was a dispatch manager when we first got married, which had me receiving calls at all hours of the night. I began sleeping on the couch with my phone under my pillow so he wouldn't wake up. Three months into the marriage, he told me I needed to quit my job because he couldn't sleep with the phone ringing and he couldn't sleep with his wife, not in the bed. I asked what I was supposed to do. I wasn't some spring chicken, and my paycheck was a large chunk of our income. His emotions always ran very high. So, I left my $60K year job because he insisted I do so. I found another job, but months into it realized there was a lot of corruption, so I told Ray I had to quit.

I do believe God allowed me to work that short-lived job for a purpose, though. One day, I was in my office, and a driver came in saying something was wrong with Fred, another one of our drivers. We all ran to the truck, and Fred was sitting behind the wheel white, with no pulse. He was D-E-A-D dead there's no mistake of this. I was on the passenger side. I started speaking in tongues and praying that man back to life. I didn't know what else to do. Right before the ambulance got there, he started moving his eyes. We didn't do mouth to mouth or CPR or anything.

Fred called me later on and thanked me. He said, "I don't know what happened, but I heard God tell me, "not today." You get to go home today. I didn't hear anything, but after God said that, I took a breath, and I heard you praying over me."

I thought that was awesome. God had me there for this purpose. Throughout that time, I was also able to witness to several co-workers. I even talked with another manager that resulted in tears running down his face. I know *that* was God. I could have focused on the negative things happening at that company and wrote my job off as something awful. However, because I focused on the many things God did while I was there, I was able to appreciate that God uses whatever He wants, whenever He wants, for His purpose.

Chapter 37

Submit to Your Husband

*I*n all my relationships, I was always the one with the house, the stuff, and the paychecks. I never had to depend on any of my partners. When Ray and I got married, we moved into my house. I had lived there nine years, so it was now the longest I had ever lived in one place. We were spending a lot of money on our daily commute since neither of us worked near the home. Six months into our marriage, Ray suggests we move into his modular home. It would drastically cut down on our commute. He even suggested we could find a church out there as well so we wouldn't have to make the hour commute to Lone Star every Sunday.

I had told him when we got married that I would not be leaving Lone Star unless God told me to do so. He could go to whatever church he wanted to go to, but that is where I would be going, even if it meant driving an hour and a half every Sunday. I had listed the house once before, and it had never sold, so I gave this listing to the Lord. If he wanted us to move, then, He needed to sell the house. We put the house up for sale on a Monday, and it sold by Wednesday. It was a bittersweet moment. It was apparent that God wanted us to move, but this was the house where I spiritually grew. I had walked the neighborhood every evening with God and my dogs, so leaving was not going to be easy.

Ray had given his tenants a thirty-day notice to vacate. He was handling that, or so I thought. On the day we had everything loaded, Ray found out they were still there just seven months into our marriage. He met the old Priscilla that night. There was no Christian in me. I had three cats, three dogs, and I told him we were

D-O-N-E done! I was going to rent another house, and he wasn't allowed to be there. Women want security, and when we don't get security, we lose it. Let's just say I wasn't the best wife that night. I made me a pallet of blankets and pillows in my walk-in closet, brought my animals in with me, shut the door, and bawled. I cried out to the Lord and reminded him that he told me to marry this man. I'm supposed to hand the keys over in the morning, and I have nowhere to go.

Ray went to his house the next morning and lost his Jesus on the tenants. What made matters even worse was they had broken things and tore up that house. I sat in the driveway staring at my new home. I felt degraded, to say the least. I had already put half my stuff in a 20x20 storage unit because the house was much smaller than mine. There's no fence, and I couldn't let the dogs out of the vehicle because the place is disgusting. I went into the house and cleaned things up as best I could, but it was not a pretty time in my life.

I was in this house that was beneath the standards I had grown accustomed to, and I didn't have a job, so I had to depend entirely on my husband for income. I'd cry every morning over my miserable situation. Months went by, and the Lord told me he would not change my circumstances until I found contentment in them. Thank you, Jesus; that's exactly what I wanted to hear. NOT.

I made Ray build me a shed in the backyard so I could bring all my stuff from the storage unit to the property. We just started getting used to married life, and the bickering started back up. He wanted to know when I was going to find a job. Funny how he asked me to leave my $60K a year job but was now concerned about me contributing to the income. He resented me for not working as if I was sitting at home eating bonbons? Clearly, he didn't understand how inadequate and bound I felt at the house. And I was defeated. I had applied for jobs, even had interviews, but nothing was opening for me.

He took on a hotshot business which required a considerable investment since he would be a contractor. I told him not to do it. I knew how much trouble it would be because of my experience being a contractor with FedEx, but he took his non-Christian friends' advice.

After living in the modular home for two years, I had finally surrendered and found contentment in my living situation. It was around this time that Ray and I decided we would move to Conroe, TX, so we'd be in the middle of our two jobs. When we began discussing what we wanted in a house, I told him I had always dreamed of a place with a porch located down a dirt road. I told him I also wanted donkeys and cows so I could watch them from the porch. When he asked why, I said, "Because I like them."

Some of our biggest struggles in marriage were due to us each wanting to do what we wanted. As I strived to adapt to my role as wife, I used to tell Ray, "Ray, God made me your helpmate; why won't you listen to me." It reminded me of King Jehoshaphat. He listened to his stupid friends instead of the elders. Ray not taking my advice made me feel awful. I was trying to be a dutiful wife and support him. Why couldn't he see that I wanted good things for him?

Since I was a stay-at-home wife who didn't work, I began facing insecurities. But all was not lost; Ray had introduced me to Chaplain Dunn. She was the prison chaplain at Plane State women's unit. Once I had gotten to know her, I asked if there were any sexual abuse bible studies in the unit. She said no and asked me to submit the entire program so she could get it approved. Several months later, in 2013, I got a promotion and began my own bible study at the women's prison. In 2015, when I was not working, Chap asked me to be one of her CVCAs-certified volunteer chaplain assistant. So, I took all the training, and once again, the Lord gave me another promotion. I was moving up from paper, pencil, and a hug!

Chapter 38

Prison Duty

I worked my butt off at that prison volunteering for eight hours a day Tuesday through Saturday. Whenever Ray would ask me when I was going to find a real job, I started saying whenever God releases me from this one. The inmates would ask me if I got paid, and when I said no, they wanted to know why I was there. I told them it was because this is the job the Lord had given me, and He would pay me back in heavenly blessings. One of Chaplain Dunn's gifts is the gift of encouragement. The first time I was with her at a prison church service, she said, "Priscilla, come up here and give them a word."

Excuse me!

I had never spoken to a crowd in ministry before, and especially not to one hundred inmates. I went up there praying, *Lord Jesus help me, speak through me.* It took me five more times before I started going to each church service prepared with a word. Then she allowed me to preach at one of the units and began encouraging me to preach more. Ray would give a 10-minute opener, and then I would preach. She allowed me to blossom that way.

One time she freaked me out, we all got to the prison; she tore up little pieces of paper and put numbers on each one of them. She had everybody pull a number out, then said, "Here is the verse. Number one, you go; first, you talk for 10 minutes, then the next number, then the next. No notes, no prep, we're just going to see what the Holy Spirit does."

That impromptu preaching taught me how to listen to the Holy Spirit and let Him have His way and His will instead of depending on myself.

Chaplain Dunn became another mentor. She would sit there and speak into my life. Darla was a mentor in growth and boundaries. Misty was a mental counselor. Chaplain Dunn was a supernatural mentor. She spoke supernatural things into my life and believed in me in that supernatural way. I was finally starting to see the things that God had in me. I could not have walked this walk and left that lifestyle without those three women speaking into my life on a regular basis. I think a lot of times, people get saved and believe this is a lone journey. Negative ghost rider. We need other women who can speak into our lives, who are not our equal. A lot of times, new Christians want to hang out with new Christians. It's ok to have your newbie friends and have lunch with them but don't allow them to speak into your life. They are just as ignorant as you are. Reach out and find the person who has been saved for 20-30 years, who is Spirit-filled and walking right with the Lord.

With these three beautiful, wonderful, mature Christian women speaking into my life all at the same time, all for different areas of my life, how could I not grow? It was impossible for me not to grow. So many times, people become stagnant ponds because they don't let life flow through, in and out of them. I always keep moving no matter how much it hurts or how many times I cried. I cried a lot during my first few years of salvation, tears of joy, confusion, fear, healing, and loss. Many people are deceived into thinking when you get saved, there are no more tears, oh you liar! It's a journey; there's no graduation. We don't get to graduate until we get to heaven. Only then are there no more tears.

Chapter 39

Into the Ministry

We were prison hoppers, and I loved it. We were at the women's prison all week, then on the weekend's Chaplain would preach at different men's units. One time Chaplain Dunn asked me if we would go with her to Hightower Prison. They had three services for the inmates, and she asked me to preach the third one. This unit was a sexual perpetrator prison; 80% of the prisoners had committed sexual assault. I had to prepare myself mentally. When Ray and I showed up, another lady from our posse was waiting in the parking lot. She said Chaplain Dunn wasn't going to make it, which meant the three of us would be handling the services.

Since I was the only one who had a decent amount of material prepared, I would have to preach all three services, but the first service was the longest. I got up there and preached my twenty-minute sermon, which God turned into thirty minutes. Halfway through the sermon, I heard God speak to me clearly, so I said, "There's somebody here that has always wanted to ask their victim for forgiveness and has never had the chance to. I was abused, and my perpetrator has never asked for me forgiveness. If you want that opportunity come up here now, and I'll stand in the gap."

At first, just one man walked up to the front, then two more. I walked up to each of them and asked what they had done and who they had harmed. Each one of them whispered their offense in my ear and, through heaving sobs, asked me to forgive them on behalf of their victim. When I got to the third man, I realized some more men had come forward about ten, and then when I looked up again, there was another ten or so. Ray and the other lady couldn't believe what was happening. The officer couldn't believe what was happening. While all this is going on, the band is playing, and the Spirit was moving; I could feel the presence of the Lord all in that place. Over fifty men that morning asked me to forgive them on behalf of their victim or victims. I was able to forgive and give forgiveness. Many tears fell that morning, mine included. By the grace of a loving Father, these men were set free. I think that was one of the most rewarding experiences that I have yet to encounter. It was precious to them and me. Those are the kind of things God has worked in me and through me.

I was in the women's prison every day, eight hours a day. My life was full of ministry, walking female inmates through the Acts of Grace program, and my volunteer Chaplain position. One Saturday, I took Pastor Darla to meet some of the offenders in my AOG class at the prison in Dayton, TX. On the way home, she asked if I wanted to be ordained like her, and I jumped on it. I started bible school in August of 2014 through Berean School of the Bible. I was immersed in this Jesus culture, this Jesus life. I saw no signs of my past- no drinking, no nothing. The further I walk with Jesus, the further my past is behind me.

The more that I set my heart and mind on following Jesus, the less I recall the person I used to be. I have memories of the past, but I don't remember actually being that person. All things have become new. I once ran into a guy; for three years, I had been his boss. I ran into him and said, "Hey, how are you doing?" He looked at me, and I could tell he didn't know who I was. I said, "It's me, Priscilla."

He said, "Why can't I recognize you? I can't see you from how I remember you. What's changed about you?"

I said, "Maybe it's because I got saved, and Jesus has transformed me. That's probably why you don't recognize me."

He said, "Man, you really don't look like the same person. You have a glow to you"

When we get saved and start the sanctification process, people should be able to tell there's something different about us.

Chapter 40

Working at Lone Star Cowboy Church

After eight months of volunteering full-time at the prison, I started praying for a job. I wanted my own job, my own paycheck. By this time, I was attending bible school and working to become an ordained minister with the Assemblies of God. But I had no idea what the purpose was in any of it. I was at this crossroad. I just didn't know what I was doing. Driving and crying. Poor pitiful me. I was coming up to a curvy part in the road and heard Him speak clear as day, "Like this curvy road ahead, you don't see what's coming around the corner, but I do, be still."

"Yes, Lord, ok." It was such a visual. It made me think of a parade. A person sitting there on the street can only see the band and floats coming to the left and leaving to the right as they are at ground level. But if you are sitting in a high-rise building, you can see everything from way off. That's how God is; He can see further than we can. I was praying every day, going on and on about wanting a job. I think He had gotten tired of me because one morning, He said, "Call Darla and ask her for the care pastor position."

I replied, "I'm not qualified."

I ignored His instruction for about a week. Then, when I began praying for a job again, He said the same thing. I told him I wasn't qualified, but later on, as I was pulling into the Kroger parking lot, he said, "CALL HER."

I prayed she wouldn't answer, but of course, she answered after the first ring. I told her God wanted me to ask her something, and then I told her what He had said. She said, "You're not qualified."

I said, "I know that's what I told Him." She asked what made me think I was qualified, and I replied, "I just told you I'm not; I don't even know what a care pastor does."

She listed off the care pastor's responsibilities, and I was surprised that I was actually already doing some of those things in the prison. She asked me to be at the office at 10 AM the following day. When I got to the office, Darla wasn't there, so I waited and waited. When I called her and told her I was at the church office, she told me they would pick me up as an intern and to go see Pam. Two months before this, I had applied as a correctional officer at the prison. The reason I had applied was because I wanted to be a prison chaplain. Chaplain Dunn had told me if I did two years as a correctional officer, I could make a lateral move to a chaplain. I wanted to be a chaplain so bad that I thought that was what God wanted for me too. Wrong!

In the intern position, I went to my first hospital visit and led the man to the Lord. Every time I went to the hospital, I was leading people to the Lord. I was having a great time visiting people. Not long after, I received a call from the prison; I got the position and would be working at Hightower Unit; the prison where the men had asked for forgiveness. I was so excited!

I told Pastor Darla I had a job and would have to put in my notice.

She said, "Don't you like it here?"

I said, "Yes, but I know you're still looking for a Care Pastor, and when you find him, I'll have to leave. I need to take this job."

A few days later, I got a call from Pastor Randy, and he wanted to offer me a job as the Care Director. Can you believe that? I had asked God for a job, and He gave me two. I called Ray and told him about both positions and asked him to pray with me about it. We decided that I should take the job at Lone Star Cowboy Church even though it was an hour and a half away; instead of going sixteen miles to the prison. So, in just two months, I went from intern to Care Director. They hired a Care Pastor in March, and I liked him, but he only lasted two weeks. I was tired of waiting for another pastor to be hired, so I just started doing things. The first thing I did was start an intercessor prayer team; they were responsible for praying over every prayer request submitted to the church. I implemented a senior living ministry, a homeless ministry, and Darla then handed over the Acts of Grace ministry to me. I was still doing hospital visits, so I also decided to implement a cancer care ministry.

In this position, I was also over church benevolence, weddings, and funerals. In June 2016, they still didn't have a Care Pastor, and I said, "God, you didn't tell me to ask for the Care Director position. You told me to ask for the Care Pastor position." And that is when I began believing it was mine. So, I worked my tail off to prove I could do the job.

When December came around, they were no longer talking about hiring a Care Pastor. I was now certified with Assemblies and was working on my license. By January 2017, I had finished all 28 courses. On March 1, 2017, I was promoted to Care Pastor and received my AG license shortly afterward. Sadly, Ray passed away on April 28, 2017. So, I started my first full year of being a pastor dealing with grief.

Chapter 41

Like a Vapor

R ay was a very funny man, and he could make people laugh all the time. He had a great personality and a beautiful smile. Beautiful blue eyes, head of white hair, and very buff and physically fit. He had such a sweet, gentle spirit. He loved Jesus and always fell asleep with the Bible on his chest. We would pray together, and I know that helped our marriage even though we had a rough start. He loved me, and I loved him.

When I got promoted to a pastor, I was ecstatic. God's prophetic word came to pass; He told me to ask for it, and it came to pass. It may have been two years before it came to pass, but at least it wasn't seventeen years like King David.

On Monday, April 24, 2017, I had a dream. Ray and I were holding hands, walking through a huge crowd. A crowd came towards us, someone came between us, and we got separated. I could see his white head through the crowd, but he kept walking away from me and eventually disappeared in the crowd. I woke up that morning and asked God what the dream meant. I asked if we were going different ways in ministry? Why are we going separate ways? We did prison ministry together. It didn't make sense.

That morning, as I was pondering on the dream, Ray asked me to sign him up for Man Camp. I told him they were leaving on Thursday, but he insisted God told him to go to Man Camp. Ray was very involved at Lone Star Cowboy Church, so it wasn't much of a surprise that Ray wanted to go. He did the Facebook live stream for first services, taught Sunday school for the fifth and sixth grades at the second service, and the third service was part of the prayer team.

On Thursday, he got off work, took a shower at the church, and got the keys to the church van. I hugged him, and a kiss goodbye told him to have a great time, and I'd see him Saturday. I didn't know that would be the last time I saw him.

The next day, I woke up ready to check off my to-do list. Ray sent me a text letting me know that he was having a good time. They made him the leader in his cabin. He was excited that I would be attending the following week for the women's camp. That was the last text I would receive from him.

My mom was going in for surgery that morning, so I called and prayed with her while I was at the car dealership to have a sensor replaced. I knew it would be a little while, so I had brought my highlighters and a book, *Pastoral Care How to Deal with Grief.* As I was sitting there, Pastor Rob's name flashed on my phone. When I answered, he immediately said, "Priscilla, don't be alarmed."

Of course, that immediately put me on high alert. Now I was alarmed. I asked what was going on, and he told me they thought Ray had just had a heart attack.

Now, before I continue, let me back up to December 2016 for a moment. The Lord kept telling me to get Ray life insurance. Honest to God truth! I got a thing in the mail for AARP, filled it out, and set it in front of Ray. When he asked what it was, and I told him life insurance, he said, "What, you think I'm going to drop dead of a heart attack?"

I said, "I hope not, but if you do, everything will be paid off."

Fast forward four months to the call I just received. I went up to the service station and told them I needed my car now; my husband might be having a heart attack. Thankfully they had just finished. As I was getting my vehicle, I got another phone call from Rob telling me to bring somebody with me. I called my sister Tammy and asked if she would go with me on the two-hour drive. Before I arrived at my sister's house, I received another text from Pastor Rob: Pray, it doesn't look good.

My sister is driving the car, and I'm in the passenger seat with high anxiety. I can't talk to my mom because she is in surgery, so I called my dad. He said, "*Mija*, it's okay. I had a triple bypass. They do good things today."

Tammy tells me to call the hospital and ask about the status of my husband. So, I did. The nurse put me on hold, and the next voice I heard was Alex Stinson. He taught Sunday school with Ray. "Alex? Is Ray dead?"

"Yes, I'm sorry, he didn't make it."

The minute I heard he was dead, that dream I had on Monday dropped on me, and I realized that is what the dream had meant. My sister pulled over to the side of the road, and we were both bawling. I told her to get off the side of the road and get to the hospital. I called Pastor Rob, and he confirmed what Alex had said. I told him we were still thirty minutes away from the hospital. When I got to the hospital, they took me to Ray; he was covered with a sheet and had his little corky smile on his face. I messed with his hair, kissed his forehead, kissed his lips, and told him I loved him.

I told the Lord I wasn't going to ask Him why; He didn't owe me an explanation. I knew Ray's death didn't pass through God's fingers without His permission. Then I told the Lord He was my husband again. The only question I did have was, "What's next? What plans do you have for me now?" Since I knew my life had just changed drastically. By 3 pm, I was sitting in a funeral home talking about my husband's remains. I now understood what the Bible meant when it told us to say *"if the Lord be willing"* and *"life is but a vapor."* (James 4:14 &15)

Ray did indeed die from a heart attack; it was one of those widow makers. He had just finished a canoe race. After standing on the dock, just a few minutes after the race, Ray collapsed and died instantly.

On the way home, I got a call requesting his body parts since he was a donor. I had to answer all these questions that nobody should have to answer, especially not in that state of mind. Walking into the house was an unreal feeling. There was nothing out of the ordinary. It was just like any other day where he was at work and not yet home. But this day, he wouldn't be coming home.

Tammy stayed with me and slept in my bed, something we hadn't done since high school. At 4:30 in the morning, I woke up and went outside. The wind was blowing like crazy. As I felt that swirl around me, I knew the Lord was wrapping his arms around me. He said, "Like these trees, you will bend, but you won't break because you are strongly rooted, and I have you."

Pastor Randy and Pastor Darla were in the mountains with no service. When they finally got word of Ray's death, they immediately drove to Man Camp and started consoling the men. They had all gone to attend this happy weekend together and had now lost a friend. Many of the men said Ray's death brought them closer to the Lord later down the road. He would have been happy to know that.

I was beginning the grieving process, but I was pretty far away from my church family. There weren't any visitors stopping by the house, but because we went to a church of 2000 people and I was one of the pastors there, I was soon bombarded with an explosion of the worst kind- Facebook, instant messenger, text messages, phone calls. Everyone telling me how sorry they were for my loss or what Ray had meant to them.

Two days after his death, I received a message from Jason Terry. He informed me that he was Ray's son-in-law. I knew about Ray's daughter Leah, but I had never met her. She hadn't seen her dad since she was fifteen and hadn't talked to him for the past eight years, but she wanted to say goodbye. They had left Florida as soon as they heard about Ray's death and were on their way to Texas but had no idea where they were going. In one weekend, I had lost my husband and instantly gained a daughter-in-law, son-in-law, and two grandkids. Because the memorial service was a week away, I got to know Leah and the grandkids. They started calling me Gammy P, which was a little overwhelming. My mom and nephew showed up. For an entire week, I was surrounded by people. About a week after the memorial service, I told my mom she had to leave. It was time for me to walk through this grief process.

Grief is strange. There were days I would be fine, and then there were days I would wind up on the floor crying. The healing process was not easy. The church was so good to me during this time. Pastor Darla told me I could come into the office just to lay on the couch and cry if I needed to. She wanted to make sure I was still around people.

I decided it was time to sell the house and get back to Montgomery to be close to work and friends. I had a realtor give me a list of everything I should fix before I listed the house, so I went to work. I planned to sell the house and buy another, but Pastor Darla and Pastor Connie both advised me against it. They recommended I rent a house. I knew I wasn't in a very good emotional state, so I listened to their advice.

Chapter 42

Remodeling My Soul

Before selling my home, I started to calculate the deposit for five pets. Although it would be steep with deposits then first and last month's rent, I knew I had to start searching for that home. Someone at church told me about a house next to their property. Nobody had lived in it for over six months, so he thought I might be able to rent it from his neighbor. I figured it couldn't hurt to look at it.

It was on the acre behind his house. We waded through the thigh-high hayfield to the little house. When we got close enough to examine the place, I thought, *Oh my word.* The screen door was broken, the sink was broken, the stove needed to be thrown away, holes in the walls; it was in bad shape, I called it "The Shack." It was built in 1941, and the entire house was only 625sqft. I said, "Wow, God, you're taking me from the palace to the pit." But as I was looking around, God gave me a vision of what the house could look like.

I asked my friend from church to take me to the landlady. She told me she would charge $300 for rent. Deposit? Nope. Pet deposit? Nope. Just $300. I asked if I could paint the house. She said that would be fine. Just take the cost off the rent. Just as

I'm about to leave, I looked up to see cows and donkeys walking across the pasture. Cows and donkeys! Not to mention, it was off of a dirt road and had a porch. God hears all our desires, even the simplest ones.

Now I had a project. When I got home from work, I would spend my evenings fixing up the modular home, and on the weekends, I would fix up the rental. I had no more time to sit around crying. Pastor Connie begged Pastor Darla to talk me out of the rental. She said I was grieving and not thinking right. But Pastor Darla said, "She's a big girl."

The arena life group from the church showed up one Saturday to check everything out on the rental. They mowed the yard and looked at everything for me: plumbing, electrical, drywall patching, and anything else they could fix that day. The women from the church came over one day, removed all the cabinets, stripped them, and repainted the whole house. For two months, I worked on this house before it could be decent enough so that I could move in. We covered the front of the house in tin, that rustic tin; a friend and I stripped all the floors and re-stained them. I had so many people come and help me with this house. It had so many cracks I filled it with can spray foam. I converted the second bedroom to a walk-in closet. I now call it my one bedroom with a walk-in closet and an on-suite.

As this house healed, I healed. It took me almost two years to make it the cute tiny home it is today. Although I have no central air and heat, no insulation whatsoever, and I only have window units. God has brought me total contentment, and this is one home I am going to truly miss. I went from being totally materialistic as a new convert to being content in what I called 'The Shack.' All the money that I would have invested into a home that required first/last month's rent plus pet deposits I spent on this shack. And it was well worth the investment for my soul.

In April 2018, I went to Cuba. It was the first time I had been exposed to the living conditions of this communist country. They were so poor but had no idea what they didn't have. Pastor Darla remembered a guy from a previous trip and came prepared with a pair of shoes. When she gave him the shoes, he cried and cried and cried because he didn't have any shoes. Right then and there, I saw a man who depends on God for everything in his life, even a pair of shoes. When I was sitting in the hotel, God said, "This is the plan I have for you."

Oh, no, no, no. I couldn't believe He was calling me to missions.

When I had moved into 'The Shack,' I put all my stuff in a 10x20 storage unit. It was stacked front to back, top to bottom: no more boats, swimming pools, or king-size beds. The materialistic me finally died! It had only taken seven years, hey sanctification can be a slow process. After the mission trip, I sat in my living room and started talking through everything with God. I have a couch, a refrigerator, a stove, and a bed. Compared to what those people in Cuba had, I had so much more. I said, "Solomon was right vanity, vanity all is vanity." I went to my storage unit and sold everything. What I didn't sell I gave away, and what I didn't give away I threw away. I was now down to the necessities. But even then, the little I still had was vanity, but I couldn't go into the mission field. I had my pets. They were old, and I loved them. I loved my tiny house. Working on it brought me joy and healing after Ray's death. The landlady had been such a blessing to me, and I was a blessing to her. And above everything else, I had my job. I had worked so hard to get this job. I was a pastor; for goodness sake, how could I just walk away from that?

From April through September 2018, I prayed and journaled. I had talked to certain people, and they encouraged me to go to the mission field, but others did not care for the idea and tried to discourage me. Let this be a lesson, don't tell everybody your stuff. Satan wants you to be confused. And I was confused on whether God called me or didn't. In September, I said I'm not going to journal about it, talk about it, or pray about it. I'm going to wait until Ray has been gone two years; going to wait until I am ordained.

In April 2019, a few weeks before the second anniversary of Ray's death, I went on another mission trip. Once again, I can feel God calling me to the mission field. I got home and told him I was sorry, but I couldn't give up my pets. He asked if my pets were more important than souls.

You really had to go there?

I'll give you my pets. I'll put them on the altar, so to speak, but You have to do whatever it is you're going to do. And He did just as He always does. He opened one door after another as He led me straight to the mission field. In August, I set an appointment with the executive pastoral staff at Lone Star and told them the Lord was calling me to missions, and I wanted their blessing.

Then, in January 2020, after a very long application process, I was invited to the missionary orientation in March. As soon as I returned, everything was shut down due to COVID. Part of the requirements for going to the mission field is raising all your own money, so I spent a good portion of last year raising money. Today I am 100% funded and leave for Costa Rica on April 29th, 2021. There I will learn Spanish and from there head to the Dominican Republic. Initially, I picked Cuba, but they asked me to go to the Dominican. I will be working with the sexually abused and those who are struggling with same-sex attractions. The Lord has never used my gay lifestyle to minister to gay people. It's been nine and a half years, and now he is going to use it.

Chapter 43

Go and Grow

⌢

This may be the end of the book, but this is not the end of the story. In 2012, I found myself struggling with temptation. I had a horrible oppression come over me, and I wanted to drink so bad. I was praying, going to church and life groups, doing everything and anything that I could to combat this urge to drink on my own. Nothing was helping. It was as if God had gone silent. I was on my way to church for a New Year's Eve bonfire when I passed a bar and heard, "Just go. Nobody will know."

I gripped my steering wheel, and I got mad. Instead of talking to God, I decided to talk to someone else. "Satan!!!" I yelled, "You are showing me the good side of that bottle. That I will have fun and relax, but you are not showing me the dark side. That I could get drunk and wind up doing something I would regret or maybe even get a DUI. I am not going to grieve the Holy Spirit. I am not going to miss prison ministry tomorrow for you." Instantly, I felt the claws come off me; I was released. I have not had the desire to drink ever since. I went toe to toe with him. I said, "Not today, not ever! You are not my master, and I don't obey you."

Isn't it interesting that I wasn't able to do the same when it came to that night with my friend? It just proves to me that some sins will be harder to resist than others. Maybe because we have struggled with them longer and found ourselves more comfortable with them. I'm not sure.

This is what I want to leave you with.

Christianity is not a walk in the park. A question that should always be at the front of a Christian's mind is, "Who am I feeding more?"

Every day we have a chance to feed our spirit or our flesh. Say your daily commute takes thirty minutes to work, then another thirty back home if you listen to secular music the entire ride. That's one hour of feeding your flesh. Then once you get home, you watch three hours of TV. That brings the count to four hours. Most people spend about thirty minutes on each meal, which brings the total up to five and a half hours.

Now, what about the spirit? Do you only go to church and never pick up your Bible or worship during the week? If so, your spirit man is dying and starving to death. Even if you pick up your Bible once a week, you're still starving.

You have to feed your spirit man more than you feed your flesh man; until your spirit man is bigger and greater than your flesh man. Your flesh does not want your spirit man to grow. Your flesh will win every battle if your spirit man is not growing and maturing. And it will do everything in its power to keep your spirit man as a newborn. Believe me, as a pastor, I have counseled people who have been saved for twenty years, and there is no growth.

Take a personal inventory and see who you feed more. The Bible tells us to die to self and pick up our cross, not once or twice but daily! Start dying to self; it will be good for you.

That's how I did it. I put more Jesus in me, fed the spirit more than my flesh. And believe me, it has not been easy. It is easy to say I don't have time today. It's easy to say I'd rather listen to this on the way to work. The easy way is to satisfy your flesh, and it feels better. But if you want to grow, then you've got to do something different.

If God can take a wretch like me and turn my life around, He can surely do the same for you.

My theme song I always play for the ladies at the end of my Acts of Grace class is "Clean" by Natalie Grant. There is a line in the song that says, "My dirty rags are purified." In everything that I went through in life, nothing made me dirtier than the unforgiveness I harbored in my heart. Some people might read through my story and say I had every right not to forgive those who caused me pain. But God says differently,

> *"If you forgive those who sin against you, your heavenly Father will forgive you. But if you refuse to forgive others, your Father will not forgive your sins." Matthew 6:14-15 (NLT)*

Can you guess the three people in my life I harbored the most unforgiveness towards? My mom, my dad, and, of course, Luis. All of them had hurt me on various levels. Even if you've never been through a situation like I was with Luis, I'm sure you can relate to the hurt I experienced with my parents. Maybe you are bitter towards your parents or another family member right now. If you remember, I actually changed my last name at one point in my life because I was so angry with my dad.

> *"Unforgiveness is like drinking poison yourself and waiting for the other person to die." –Marianne Williamson*

This quote is one thousand percent true. Forgiveness has to be something we choose to walk in. It's not like when you're little, and your parents tell you to say sorry to your sibling, and you grudgingly say you're sorry but don't mean it. God knows our hearts. We can't fool Him like we fooled our parents. We can't say, "I forgive them," and secretly not forgive.

My dad was the first that I forgave. And this was back before I was saved. The fifth step of AA required me to make amends in my life. Debbie, my sponsor, let me make some of those amends through letters and phone calls, but she was insistent that I had to make amends with my dad in person. She said, "You apologize for your actions and behavior, and don't worry if he doesn't apologize. You're not responsible for his side of the street; you're responsible for yours."

It had been four years since I changed my name. So, I drove five hours to see him and ask for forgiveness. When I did, he hugged me, told me he loved, and assured me there was nothing to forgive. We visited for a little while that day, and he never once said he was sorry or asked for forgiveness in return. But just as Debbie had said, I was not responsible for his side of the street, so I didn't give it a second thought. I left his house that day without a single ill-feeling towards my dad. A few years ago, he did ask me to forgive him for not being the dad I needed him to be.

Next was my mother. I had been saved for a couple of years; I had gone through Acts of Grace and counseling, so I thought everything was forgiven between us. But every time I spoke with her, I was snippy and rude. There were times when she would ask me why I was so rude to her, but I really didn't know. I had no idea how deeply bitterness was rooted down into my heart. So, one day I asked God if he would show me why I was acting this way.

A week later, I received an email from Debbie, my AA sponsor. She told me that she had found my paper from step four in a briefcase. She asked if I wanted her to burn it (she knew me so well) or send it to me. I told her to go ahead and send it to me. When I received that envelope, it was as if God himself had mailed me the answer to my prayer. This paper that she had found after almost thirteen years contained everything I held against my mom. Every hurt that I held against her.

As I read through the letter, I began to cry. Then my mom called me. She asked what I was doing, and I told her I was reading a letter about her. She asked me to read it to her, but I told her she wouldn't want to hear it. She said, "Well, let me pray. Lord, help me to be receivable for what I am about to hear."

I read her everything I had written in that letter, and she was crying, "wow, I was a horrible mother. Will you forgive me?"

I had a split second to decide if I was going to forgive her and never hold anything against her from that day forward. So, I made the choice, "yes, mom, I forgive you." The next day, I was driving, and I said, "Wow, Lord, I can never hold anything from my past against her again." And I haven't.

Forgiving Luis was a bit more of a process. After going through Acts of Grace and counseling, I began praying for him; for his salvation. After I had been saved for seven years, I received a phone call from my brother Louie who was now in prison. He said, "Priscilla, I need you to call my dad and have him wait for my call. I know I'm asking a lot from you, but I wouldn't ask if I had another option."

I hadn't spoken to Luis since I was nineteen years old. When he answered the phone, it was as if God had disguised his voice. I said, "Luis, Louie needs you to call him."

He said, "Tammy?"

I ignored his question and said, "Louie is going to call you. Can you be by the phone?"

He asked, "Is this Tammy?"

I said, "No, it's Priscilla."

For a moment, there was silence. Then he said, "Oh." Followed by, "I pray for you."

I replied, "I pray for you too."

It was around Christmas, and he replied, "Have a good Christmas."

Before I hung up, I asked, "Do you know what Christmas is about? Jesus came and died for our sins for you and for me. Have a Merry Christmas."

At that moment, I hung up the phone when I realized I no longer had any unforgiveness towards Luis. I thanked God for the healing He had provided.

> *"You have heard the law that says, 'Love your neighbor' and hate your enemy. But I say, love your enemies! Pray for those who persecute you! In that way, you will be acting as true children of your Father in heaven. For he gives his sunlight to both the evil and the good, and he sends rain on the just and the unjust alike." Matthew 5: 43-45 (NLT)*

Forgiveness is not something that magically happens in a moment. It is something we must allow God to work through us. I continue to pray for Luis's salvation that he would get saved and go to heaven. I do this because Jesus laid it out as a requirement, not an option.

As we part ways, I encourage you to look up "Clean" by Natalie Grant and allow the lyrics to wash over you. God knows where you have been, and He knows where you are going. Invite Him to be a part of the journey.

A Note from the Author

During the two years of counseling I went through at Lone Star Cowboy Church, there was an exercise that I was asked to complete. I had to write, sing, or choose a song. Whatever I did, it had to be creative to show where I was and where I am today. I wrote out the following poem. This poem is what inspired me to write this book.

> *Happy childhood in the beginning*
> *Then came adultery with a very bad ending.*
> *Daddy's come and daddy's go*
> *They even let their babies go.*
> *With divorce no one wins*
> *Satan comes and pours out sin.*
> *Daddy's women come and go*
> *He teaches his children it's just a show.*
> *Mom just as selfish on her end*
> *For the men she brings home causes nothing but*
> *pain and sin.*
> *A child frighten in the dark*
> *She knows tonight the abuse with start.*
> *Abuse goes on year after year*
> *Must she continue to live in fear?*
> *Innocents lost shame has won*
> *Alcohol is now number one.*

The Impossible Change

Booze and drugs are out of hand
Neither parent gives a damn.
Teenage years are full of destruction
Nothing but a life of corruption.
Sex is now in full swing
And because of her examples it's no big thing.
Sleep with him, sleep with her
Who really cares nothing hurts.
A baby is conceived and then discarded
What does it matter the life never started.
The pain is real, it's so far down
Only alcohol can turn this around.
Women are now a desire of the heart
They were comfortable from the start.
Now the women come and go
This looks the same as daddy's show.
There is something missing in this life
And His name is Jesus Christ.
Deep inside she has no hope
So, she continues to hide in the dope.
God and church are not an option
For long ago they were part of her corruption.
She can do this on her own
Living life on her throne.
Years go by and nothing changes
Except God had a plan and moved her to Texas.
Still living deep in sin
God reaches out and pulls her in.
Not so sure of what's going on
She accepts the Lord and presses on.
Things are changing in her life
And it's only because she received Jesus Christ.
Her sins are forgiven and she's finally set free
Because only in Christ is there victory.
Act of Grace to deal with the abuses

Bible in tow is what she chooses.
Acts of Grace to deal with the abortion
Thank you, Jesus, for restoration.
Wednesday after Wednesday she sat with the church counselor
To put back her life that was full of disaster.
Layer after layer the onion was peeled
Then one day she could finally feel.
Lessons were learned at those weekly meetings
That her life really had purpose and meaning.
The chains were broken one link at a time
Because God had told her "you will always be mine".
Through fire and trials and storms that blew
It was the promises of His word that helped her through.
When Satan comes knocking with old behaviors
There's not much he can do since she has her Savior.
Now her life is full of joy and peace
And she received it all upon her knees.
Women are still much a part of her life
But only now they are sisters in Christ.
So just when you think there is no hope
Just look up above to our King, Lord of Host!!

By Priscilla Navaroli

CPSIA information can be obtained
at www.ICGtesting.com
Printed in the USA
FSHW021117100321

9 781662 813290